No Longer Hostage

Sharonda Jones

Little Phoenixes Publishing
UPPER MARLBORO, MARYLAND

Copyright ©2021 by Sharonda Jones.

All rights reserved. No part of this publication may be reproduced, distributed or transmitted in any form or by any means, including photocopying, recording, or other electronic or mechanical methods, without the prior written permission of the publisher, except in the case of brief quotations embodied in critical reviews and certain other noncommercial uses permitted by copyright law. For permission requests, write to:

>Sharonda Jones
>d.b.a. Little Phoenixes Publishing
>Post Office Box 7241
>Upper Marlboro, Maryland 20792
>Website: www.SharondaJones.me
>Email: info@sharondajones.me

Publisher's Note: This is an autobiographical non-fiction, yet some names and details have been changed to protect the privacy of those involved.

Book Layout ©2017 BookDesignTemplates.com
Cover Photo by Clark Bailey Photography

Unless otherwise indicated, all Scripture quotations are from the New King James Version of the Bible. Copyright ©1982 by Thomas Nelson, Inc. Used by Permission.

No Longer Hostage/ Sharonda Jones. -- 1st ed.
ISBN 978-0-9992380-2-8

To those who were once hostages and have gone on to liberate others, our work will never be in vain.

To the friends who laughed, cried, prayed, carried my load, and planned secret capers with me, God blessed me when He made you.

To the storms that come my way, I am your master.

Contents

Introduction ix

Envy of My Eye 1

Still Waters 29

Where Are You? 59

My Pleasure 91

12 Years A Wife 121

Epilogue 143

Introduction

The older I get, the more I love to watch rain fall. After a hard downpour, I am reminded how important water is for growth, renewal and rejuvenation. Watching the droplets fall down the window glass, I reflect on the things I did before the rain fell, and what I look forward to doing once it subsides. I seldom take the time to do this when the weather is nice; too busy being busy, I suppose. Then the world came to a halt under the weight of a global pandemic, and everyday felt like a rainy day. I was forced to see what I thought were raindrops falling in my life for what they really were; forced to take heed and ponder where I needed to grow, what needed to be pruned and where I needed to replant myself to survive. I was forced to admit the raindrops were a representation of my tears.

While I tend to operate as a rescuer for others, this time I needed rescuing. My periods of sadness, marked by a hard downpour of tears, were always followed by a mantra that I forced myself to accept: "I did this to myself, I must endure it." Reflecting on those moments now, I recognize the little girl in the shadows. Whenever my mom would discipline me, she would say, "You made me do this." Whenever a man would hurt me, he would say, "You made me do this." I was the cause of my pain, and I had to endure it.

Until the day came, when I finally said, "I have had ENOUGH!" There is no way my God has spared me from destruction to live in fear, confined to the decisions I made while afraid to want more. I made the choice to no longer be a hostage to anything that God has not purposed for my life, and that includes family bonds, friendships, positions, and even my marriage. Each of us has been given the free will to decide the way to live our lives. The enemy wants us to believe change is a sign of confusion, discord, or misdirection. But this is not true. Change is inevitable, and growth is too. If God did not want us to see the value in change, He would have never made our world dependent upon seasons. Renewal is based on the changes we make to be stronger and better than before.

I believe God gives us time for introspection and examination, and the enemy wants us to waste that time being busy. We often miss or fail to intentionally take the time to look deep within ourselves to determine what we must change to be the person we want to be, the person we need to be in order to live out our divine purpose. This may sound strange but the way we live can be a distraction in life. Jesus said, "I came so that you may have life and have it more abundantly." I realize we all must work in some capacity, take care of home and others, but to have a life that is abundant requires truly taking care of your spirit, mind and body.

I decided nothing shall distract me from achieving the growth I need for the next level of self-acceptance, love and peace. Divorce forced me to learn to do things on my own. I had to get a sense of vacationing alone, fending for myself, and caring for my own needs. I needed to see that I can do it without my ex-husband's help, support or permission. Occasionally, the loneliness was too deep to bear. The emptiness and tremendous sense of failure rose up inside of me and became too great. I knew we were unhappy, and I also knew the likelihood anything would change, and remain changed, was slim. It seemed promising, at first. Then our lives came to a halt and, confined to our homes under the fear of COVID-19, we were face to face with one another, our unresolved issues and unable to keep our disdain veiled.

One question I am often asked is how am I still able to smile and laugh after it all. My closest friends would say I sometimes need a swift kick in the rear to walk in optimism but, for the most part, I am generally a hopeful person. Ironically, it is the pain I have been through that allows me to be as hopeful as I am. I choose to see how far God has brought me and all that He kept me from going through as a blessing. I could focus on the idea of what type of life I could have lived, where I could have gone if I had more resources available to me, or even how different my life would have been if I had the family that I longed for growing up, but it would be grossly ungrateful for me to focus only on what was not, rather than the good that was.

Sure, I grew up without a relationship with my father or a father figure in the home. But that also means I grew up without a physically abusive father or one who made me feel daily as if I was worthless.

Sure, my mom abandoned me when I was a young girl, often leaving me with friends. But that also means I avoided the foster system and was spared from far worse conditions.

Sure, there were people I encountered with ill-intentions that brought about tremendous pain for me. But I am still here today, strong enough to share my story with you so that must count for something. What was set to hurt me only helped me to see the strength I have in me. The trials were not the source of my strength, I was already strong by the power and strength of God in me.

It has been a few years since the release of my first book *Nevertheless: Peace In Spite Of Pain* and I will admit I struggled to believe there was another book in me to write. Granted, I understood with each new day that we have life lies another opportunity for love lead the way, but with the depth of me poured into *Nevertheless*, I imagined there was nothing left to share. But I was mistaken. *No Longer Hostage* is my story of what happens not just after the pain, but rather when you free yourself from those issues that cause pain in the first place. It serves as my reminder to be strong and courageous, as scripture directs us to be.

Do not fear or be in dread of them, for it is the Lord your God who goes with you. He will not leave you or forsake you.

Deuteronomy 31:6 ESV

It is my hope that my story will remind you how important it is to see your life as a series of seasons. This includes the people in your life as well as the activities you commit to from day to day, from year to year. We can get weighed down and, to some degree, bound by our ideas of how our life should be that we miss out on an abundance of peace, wellness and joy. I pray my story will serve as a testament to the healing power of forgiving yourself and the restorative power of God's grace in the midst of picking up the pieces. God is always with us, through our pain and in our triumph, He is there.

One of the harsh realities I had to confront was recognizing that I wanted Him to bless the mess that I put myself in, but it was His grace that allowed me to see the areas where I tried to maintain control while praying for His will to be done. As a believer, I have to accept the way of love even when it feels like I am losing. For it is faith in God that we come to know the truth, which is we win, regardless of how it may seem.

When we choose love and extend love by any means necessary, we are no longer hostage to the pain of the past. We are no longer hostage to unforgiveness, guilt or shame. When we choose to understand our differences while appreciating our uniqueness, we grow in love and are no longer hostage to insecurity or envy. It is freeing to know God's love is powerful, healing, and more than enough to conquer the hurt we feel from others. We have fallen short in our lives, and it is when we understand our neighbor, friend, family has also fallen short, that we can begin to heal. I choose to no longer be hostage to the expectations others have on me and equally choose to no longer hold others hostage to my expectations. I am powerful. I am beautiful. I am valuable. I am love. I am free to be the ME God created me to be.

Are you ready?

"As I walked out the door toward the gate that would lead to my freedom, I knew if I didn't leave my bitterness and hatred behind, I'd still be in prison."

- Nelson Mandela

Envy of My Eye

"Are you jealous of her?" The question shocked me but not as much as who my soon-to-be ex-husband was accusing me of being envious.

"Why would I be jealous of my own daughter?" I responded confused and irritated at the same time.

I am not sure if I have ever truly envied anyone. Well, not in a Cain murdering Able, or Joseph's brothers plotting to kill him kind of way. Of course, I longed to have the same advantages that others had in life, a father, a childhood home, a trust fund, etc., but I never resented others for their blessings, grace or personal achievements. As far as I was concerned, carrying long-term jealousy in my heart toward others required more energy than I wanted to give. This made the idea of being jealous of the child I gave birth to, nurtured, and provided a life better than I could have ever dreamed for myself to, was beyond absurd. Everything she has access to, I sacrificed what I wanted to give her. My marriage was included in those sacrifices. I was more shocked that he refused to see the ridiculousness of me being jealous of my daughter than the fact that he posed the question to me at all. Perhaps more for reaction or to trigger an emotional outburst from me, he questioned if I envied her for their closeness because I wanted him to myself. It was obvious he cared for her, possibly more than he did for me; but considering she was his first biological child, I shrugged it off as new parent excitement. As the years went by, I could no longer ignore how he greeted her first when he got home from work, spent hours talking with her, or made sure to include her on road trips to his hometown. She became his little bestfriend and I was just her mother. To his credit, I did not necessarily complain either. My life was full of other responsibilities, from being a parent to my two other children, starting a non-profit organization and writing my first book. I also worked and made time for my favorite activity, riding my motorcycle, whenever possible. I admit, we grew apart. I want to say we stopped having fun together, but honestly, I struggle to remember a time when it was just the two of us. Our time together always included my children. This was one of the main reasons I rushed to get married. He was there for them and wanted to be. Sure, we would go out once and a while, but because we worked in the same building, it felt as if we spent more than enough time together. In hindsight, we failed to spend time together as a couple, getting to know one another and securing our foundation as a unit for when the storms and rain would come our way. I knew his love for our daughter was beginning to fill the void created by the connection we lost as a couple, but as for me being jealous of her…perhaps, but not for the reason he assumed.

She has a dad who loves her. Watching them gave me, for the first time, a glimpse into the unconditional love of a father for his daughter. I did not envy her for his love of her, it was his love for her that reminded me of a love I would never know.

When I tell people I am an only child, usually the first thing they say is, "Oh, you're spoiled." The older I got, the more this irritated me. Pray for me, because it still does today. I understand, in a perfect world, an only child would expect to receive their heart's desires without having to share their parents' affection or gifts of love with anyone else. My ex-husband was his mother's only child and her parents' only grandchild. In my opinion, because of the love he received, the picture of someone with a spoiled upbringing fits him more than it did me. I may not have been required to share but only because there was little, if anything, to share. Not surprisingly, it is easy for others to view my life through lenses framed by their unique life choices and experiences. This includes individuals with siblings who wish they were their parents' only child.

I will admit, while being grateful for what others had done and given to me, I still longed for what I lacked. I wanted something different. Impossible to guarantee it would be better, I hoped it would be different. My childhood was overshadowed by this guilt, the guilt of wanting more. When I lived with grandma Toots, the woman who unofficially adopted me as one of her grandchildren, I had food to eat and a roof over my head, and yet I yearned to be with my mom who left me and the father who never knew me. Ignoring the guilt, I could not wait to escape from the childhood that was my reality. I have been warned about the grass not being greener on the other side but how would a child come to understand what this means. For the majority of my 45 years, I desired to know the man who left my mom to raise me on her own. The resentment for his absence I transferred to her for not giving me the life I wanted, one with my dad in it. Though I longed to know him, his absence gave room to a fantasy father, one looking for me and who had room in his heart for me. I imagined meeting him one day, running to his open arms with both of us failing to hold back the tears. Elated, he would have a thousand questions about my life and a million apologies for not being present. With everything I believed my life lacked, I could not imagine anyone wanting the life that I viewed as not enough.

Imagine barely having the love of one parent and being envied by those who grew up with love from both of their parents. Imagine being judged for making tough decisions to give my children what I went without by those who had more than enough to give. I never considered myself as better than anyone else and yet even with all I felt was missing from my life, some treated me as if I thought I did. In actuality, it is not me, they envy, it is my ability to forgive and be hopeful that they secretly covet. Often those who are willing to forgive are considered as weak. Who would be willing to admit to wanting to be someone who everyone else sees as insignificant or vulnerable? But forgiving others for the wrong they have committed against you, and walking in love towards them, requires an enormous amount of strength. It is easy to be upset with someone, to let them know you want nothing more to do with them or to tell them about themselves, but what happens after that? What reward is there for either of you? The answer: none.

Recently, I completed a personality assessment offered by an employer. The results were not surprising. According to Dr. Shirzad Chamine, creator of the Positive Intelligence assessment, I have a pleaser type personality. Challenged with expressing my needs directly, I create situations where care or concern is more of an obligation rather than a choice. Constantly in fear that I come off as ungrateful or selfish, I work overtime to show appreciation. Insisting that my needs are met or demanding what I want in a relationship may be difficult and, as a result, I suffer in silence rather than assert my non-negotiables onto others. A friend once described me as unassuming. Perhaps this is what she meant. While it was not necessary to read any further to know this report had me pegged, it continued with two additional and equally on-point personality traits.

Combined with being a pleaser, I am also an avoider. Initially, I thought it was odd to be both someone who wants to please others and someone who wants to avoid them but, as I read more, I came to understand how the two contrary extremes could be perfect accompaniments. As an avoider, I work to avert conflict with others by agreeing to things contrary to what I want, which is in essence pleasing others even if it causes me discomfort. In avoiding difficult conversations, I tend to downplay what is important to me. This is hard to maintain emotionally and explains many of my life's upheavals. The battle between what I need or want, and the subconscious tendency to silently surrender, fostered my uncertainty and insecurities. I learned to be numb to the abuse and mistreatment I received, which began when I was a young girl and continued into adulthood. Eventually, for an avoider and pleaser, the burden becomes too great, and self-preservation then becomes a priority. Hence, my tendency to run away from difficult situations.

The third trait according to the profile assessment was that of the stickler. Learning to become a perfectionist began when I was a child but not for academic reward. I wanted to be perfect for the attention and acceptance that came along as a result. In school, the two groups of children who received the most attention were those who were studious and well-behaved, and those who were incredibly defiant. If I wanted the attention of the adults in my life, I needed to stand out. Between those two choices, the good student role seemed more promising. It also avoided the threat of my mom killing me and dismembering my body like the animals she sacrificed as ritual offerings to the gods. When some parents say, "I brought you into this world and I'll take you out", it is a hollow threat. But with my mom, I feared she meant it.

Perfection meant being seen. Those who hated me, hated me because of how well I did in school. Those who loved me, loved me for the same reason, or so I told myself. As a child, adults favored me for being a good girl. Before leaving me in the care of others, my mom would say, "Be a good girl Sharonda." I tried to do as she demanded until one day I decided it was no longer worth it. The internal war began when I realized being her "good girl" was not enough to make her be the mother I needed. The girl who adults tolerated became the not-so-good girl who received a different kind of attention. I wanted to be desired. I wanted the attention I saw other girls receiving. Similar to how social media influencers are coveted for the lives they share online, I envied girls of my generation for the lives they seemed to live without knowing what it took for them to live them, or if what I saw was worth having.

My life had little value to me because I felt it had little value to those who were meant to protect and love me. As my body changed, and my hormones and emotions were either on a rollercoaster ride to hell or to Disney World, my mother's absence was felt deeply. Not that I am an expert in child psychology, but I have learned from my own children that they simply want to be comfortable in our presence. As parents, we want them to be positioned for greatness, and not merely for what their young, still maturing minds deem comfortable. We often misunderstand one another but that is the nature of parenting, show and tell. Show them how to behave while telling them, over and over again, what to do. Of course, throw in a lot of listening, care and affection, but for the most part, prepare to repeat what you already told them.

To my children, I came off as overbearing and clueless to what was important. To me, my children would never understand my sacrifice to give them a better life, even if it required spending more time away from home than I wanted. As a teenager, I did not understand my mom's decision to leave me with others. It was not until I had to make the same decision that I began to comprehend her dilemma. Eventually, I learned to see avoiding those tough conversations about what we needed from another would produce the same fruit of abandonment prevalent in my life in my children's lives. The enemy wins when we fail to recognize that while the packaging may be different, the tactics to steal, kill and destroy are nothing new. If not careful, I would direct and star in my own version of my mom's story.

My mom was not only a single parent, but she also remained my only parent. She never remarried and I can count on one hand the number of relationships I have been aware of. The only help she received with raising me was from other mothers whom she formed friendships. Absent from my life was a father figure or male role model to show me the devoted love of a father, protector and guide, and yet I resolutely convinced myself I could find a man to replace what was missing. Not knowing or having a relationship with my dad was one issue, but the consistent absence of my mom for much of my childhood magnified the void his absence created. Unfortunately, by the time I was able to decipher how a man is supposed to fit into my life, and I into his, the wall of self-preservation against abuse had already been built.

My original birth certificate indicates I was born in Charlotte, North Carolina, but what is peculiar about my birth certificate is the man listed as my father; he was her husband when she gave birth to me, but he was (in my Maury Povich voice) not the father. By the time she met my biological father, her estranged husband Eddie Watts, had been out of her life for more than five years. I doubt Eddie ever knew he was listed as my dad by default. Imagine if birth records were handled this way today, where regardless of paternity, a husband would be listed as the father of his wife's child whether or not he was present to confirm it. I entered this world with two fathers, one biological and one listed as the legal parent, but would never be able to call on either to protect me from the boogeymen who came along the way. Interestingly, I made excuses for both men because it helped me to process being alone, vulnerable and unprotected. I told myself they been robbed of the opportunity to be a father to me. There was a legitimate reason for Eddie's absence. Unaware of my existence, I felt he was not responsible for another man's baby even if he was still legally married to the mother. Excusing my biological father required a little more creativity. Instead of faulting the man who shared the responsibility of creating me, I resented the person I felt was the cause of his absence, my mom. By her account, toward the end of her pregnancy my father proposed marriage, more out of obligation than love. Proud and determined to prove she could stand on her own, she declined the proposal. I felt she caused a divide in our family before our family had a chance to form. I would be lying if I said I never wondered about the life I would have had if she said yes, or if he was allowed to be in my life, but those wonderings served no purpose in overcoming the obstacles I faced in life. In fact, the fixation I had on my dad's absence and the fantasy of him loving me, not only created emotional hurdles for me to overcome, but also caused strife between my mom and me. Eventually, that fixation would also affect my relationships with men.

I dreamed of finding my biological father but with little information from my mom, I resigned myself to it never happening. What was the likelihood that I would find the one James Johnson, Jr., a former marine visiting Charlotte, North Carolina in 1974, who met up with my mom, Shirley Mae at a local bar? If he was not looking for me, the odds that I would find him were slim, if he wanted to be found. I wondered what made my friends who lived with their fathers or had father figures in their lives different from me. Why did their fathers believe they were worth loving and mine did not? If he was not searching for me, what made him make such a decision? When I became a mother, and my own children were abandoned by their fathers, I carried the burden of their absences as well. Instead of placing the responsibility on the men who fathered my children, I placed the blame on me. I must have done something to push them away. It had to be me because it began with me when my dad left before I was born. I felt not only was I not worth staying around for, but I was not enough for another man to ever receive me as his daughter. Not once did I look at the absence of a father figure in my life as my parents' decision from a position of their own internal struggles. I viewed it as something inherently wrong with me. I became a hostage not only to their absence but also to feelings of worthlessness and abandonment. These feelings sparked my tendency to self-sabotage through avoidance, and an unhealthy need to please others. As I got older, I began to see the similarities in the men I chose and how they were representations of the father I longed to know. While I learned to see how my insecurities had created a hostage environment for me, I failed to see I was already in a hostage situation by nature of birth. My mother suffered from the same entrapment by the decisions of her mother and the abandonment she endured as a child.

My mom's father was an absentee parent as well; but unlike me, she had no one to turn to for answers. Raised by a woman who was not her biological mother with no record of an official adoption, my mom believes she was a home birth after an unplanned pregnancy. She would often tell me the story told to her. Her biological mom and the woman who would raise her were friends. When her mom decided she was not able to raise her, she asked the friend to take on the responsibility. The friend was married and raised my mom along with children of her own. My mom suffered abuse in the dysfunctional home, but now as an adult, she still longed for a connection with them. I recognize, after going through my own storms of abuse, her desire for what was familiar outweighed the need for establishing and maintaining healthy boundaries.

My mom decided to create an account on Ancestry.com to not only find her birth family, but to also locate the family who raised her. I decided I would do the same. No judgement here, but while I hoped to find information about my dad or his side of my family tree, I also wondered if the DNA test would prove my speculation that my mom was not my biological mother. Growing up, she would constantly tell me my spirit chose her to bring me into the world. I would imagine baby spirits milling through a catalog of potential parents looking for the ideal ones to call mom and dad. *"Why on earth,"* I would say to myself, *"would I pick this life."* The results of the DNA test confirmed she is my mom.

Years went by and nothing. I had forgotten about the test until one day I received an email telling me there was a DNA match to someone on my dad's side. I was in disbelief. Staring back at me was the name of someone who could lead me to my father. This was the closest I had ever been to finding the elusive James Johnson. I sent the contact a message and waited. Weeks went by but no response. While I waited, I began researching the family tree belonging to this DNA match. To my surprise, there it was listed not once but twice: James Johnson, Sr. and James Johnson, Jr. Based on the age of James Sr., I knew he had to be my grandfather, and his wife, RosaLee Berryman Johnson, my grandmother. All this time, I thought my 'James Johnson' was a fake name because of how general it was. From there, armed with this new information, the next stop in my super sleuth search was Google.

RosaLee Berryman Johnson had recently been in the news. She was not only alive but was recognized for beating the COVID-19 virus at 95 years old. *"So, she's a bad ass"*, I thought. Not even the coronavirus could take out my grandma. The news report listed several family members and shared a picture of a ZOOM meeting showing the faces of her son and several grandchildren. From there, I went on a crazed internet search frenzy. Everything I learned years before in paralegal school about background checks and conducting people searches was beginning to pay off. My research showed that my father lives in Texas, where my mom told me he was from, and he has four children. I wanted to tell Google the correct number of children is five. The more I searched, the more obsessed I became with him. Next stop, Facebook and Instagram to search for each name listed as his sibling. On social media, I found his wife, two of his siblings and several cousins. I sent messages to an aunt and a cousin and hoped someone would be brave enough to respond. His wife's page was locked but I fought the rising urge to send her a message. Each time I thought about what would I say to her, my heart ached for us both.

In the meantime, while I waited for my father's relative to respond to my messages via Ancestry.com, I decided to go digging around my mom's side of the tree. I entered her birthname, Shirley Mae in the search field and a death notice appeared. My mom's name was listed as one of the surviving children of Doris Jackson Pratt. Learning my mom's mother died before I was born was not a surprise. Seeing her name listed among other names who were her siblings was. Surviving *children*? My mom told me the same story for my entire childhood. She was given up by her mom and raised by someone else, born without record of her birth and without siblings. I believed her when she said she had no information about her birth family or how to find anyone she was related to. I never imagined finding out this was untrue. I never pressed her on the issue because of how painful the subject seemed to be for her. But this notice from Ancestry.com would not go ignored. I wanted answers and now I had a position from which I could get them. First, I had to see if any of this was real. Back to Facebook I went. This time to search for her sister and brother, my aunts and uncle. I could not believe years of longing for an extended family of my own, wishing I had family reunions to attend, or people to share a family history with was unnecessarily expended. But not just that, this family I wanted was being kept from me by someone I loved and trusted. I felt betrayed and deeply hurt. My mom knew my experiences when I was left to the care of others, and the disgust they expressed that I was forced on them like a plague. I could not understand why she would keep an entire family from me, but instead of focusing on what I had missed out on, I decided to reach out to them and make up for lost time.

Through Facebook, I was able to connect with one cousin who then opened the door for me to connect with the rest of the family. Within a few days of reaching out to her, we were all on a video conference call meeting one another for the first time. I sat and watched as my mom recognized the faces and the names of her siblings. I listened as my cousins referred to my mom as aunt. It was beyond anything I could have hoped for, but it did not stop there. They wanted to meet me in person just as much as I wanted to meet them. Turns out, they had been looking for my mom and it was the hope of one of my aunts before she passed that we would reunite. I was speechless.

In that moment, I felt as if a flower that I carried for 45 years, watered, and prayed for finally bloomed. And as expected, it was the most beautiful display I had ever witnessed. A few weeks later we took a trip to Charlotte, North Carolina for my first family reunion. It was a weekend that will live on forever in my heart. I was overcome by the heartfelt welcome from people I had just met but were genuinely happy to see us. The Charlotte crew, which is the nickname I gave them, did not want anything from me and only wanted to share their love with me. The reunion of my mom and her siblings, and introduction of me to my family changed me forever. That weekend was filled with love, acceptance, and forgiveness. In hindsight, I realize why God allowed me to connect with these family members before connecting me with the other side of my family tree. I would need their love and acceptance to soften the blow of rejection I would soon receive from my father.

On July 22, 2020, four months to the day after reaching out to the DNA matches on my father's side, I received a response. Turns out, the person who took the test was his aunt. The email was short and straight to the point,

"Sharonda,
What is your relation to James C. Johnson? Do you have Berryman ancestry and where do you live?"

I answered the questions and waited. I sent two additional messages before receiving a response. Perhaps the time it took for her to respond was spent reaching out to my father to check if my claims were valid. The final message I received through the website was a positive one. She acknowledged the likelihood that we were related as indicated by the results and offered to speak on the phone.

I did it, I found my father!

I was ecstatic and could barely contain myself for what I imagined would come. We talked for over an hour and she shared with me the history of their family, which was now my family history. We marveled over how much I had in common with many of them. Many were artists, strong academically in math and science, and several of them were writers as well. My grandfather was a master electrician, which is the same field my son has chosen. It is hard for me to put into words how wonderful it felt to have a sense of self and belonging. Now, I knew where many of my personality and hereditary traits originated.

While I loved receiving the information she shared with me, it was not lost on me that she still had not mentioned connecting me to my father. Not once did she mention whether or not she spoke with him about me, nor did she offer to share any pictures of my father with me. Instead, I received pictures of her family. Did she really think I was going to stop looking now that I was this close to him? Did she think sharing their long extensive family history and ancestral lineage with me would suffice? I hoped not.

Finally, I got up the courage to ask her if she spoke with him and she said yes. She acknowledged he did not share my enthusiasm for this long awaited meeting, and was not prepared to face the daughter who had tracked him down after all these years.

Wait. What? He wasn't ready? Who did he think he was?

I lived my entire life obsessing over him. For years, I dreamed of this day, imagined a life that could have been, and prepared myself to forgive him when he welcomed me with open arms. Finding out he wanted nothing to do with me was a crushing blow. I could sense the rage building inside me.

He can't possibly think I am going to remain a secret. If he thinks I'm going to sink back into the shadows to protect his perfect life, his perfect family, then he has another thing coming. I refuse to remain hidden any longer! I want what he owes me and no matter what, I'm going to get it.

Sorry for your luck, James, if you thought I was going to stop now. Tell your wife and kids your daughter is coming and I'm coming pissed.

Wounded, I was overcome by the flood of an unfamiliar emotion: aching jealousy. I wanted him to pay for attempting to isolate himself from me. His cowardice was ruining my fantasy of a glorious reunion, and I could not comprehend why he made this decision. Did he have money that he was afraid I wanted, or status and reputation that he feared acknowledging me would ruin? Who was he to deny me? He was not an authority figure in my life so why did he think I would obey him or his wishes? If he would not talk to me, then I would find his children. That will teach him to ignore me.

Who had I become?

Most people probably would have stopped there, but not me. I learned his daughter started a women's empowerment group on Meetup.com. I joined it and RSVP'd for the upcoming meeting. Since it was a ZOOM meeting, I would not only get to see her face but also interact with her from the comfort of my home. I had become a real-life stalker. Envy had taken a hold of me. I excused my spurious behavior with innocent curiosity and ignored the potential to cause her pain in front of a virtual group of people. Mindful of what I said, I went through with the meeting, responding to questions and trying to explain why I wanted to join a group of women located in Texas when I lived in Maryland. I lied. In fact, I told a bunch of untruths that evening. Making matters worse was the fact that my half-sister was disarmingly sweet. Her personality radiated positivity through the screen. I felt like crap. The idea that she created this forum to help women and I was using it for other motives did not sit right with my spirit. At the end of the meeting, I sent her a message asking if I could speak with her offline. She sent me her phone number and email address.

Could this woman be any sweeter?!

I sent her an email explaining who I was and prayed she would understand and forgive me. Her reply proved she was as kind as I perceived her to be and on top of that, she accepted me as her sister. We talked for almost an hour and she promised to share the news with her brothers. Correction, our brothers. Before speaking with her parents, she wanted to pray about her approach, which I understood completely. We shared pictures of our children and she acknowledged how much I resembled our dad. This is something my mom used to tell me growing up, and I had no choice then but believe her since I looked nothing like her. I assumed there was also the chance that I looked like my birth mother, since I somewhat speculated I might have been kidnapped at birth. That was until the DNA test debunked that suspicion.

After the talk with my sister, I called my mom and apologized to her for putting a man who rejected his responsibility on a pedestal instead of treasuring the woman who accepted hers. I apologized for blaming her for his absence when it turned out he never wanted to be present. Sure, our lives were not perfect, but they had not destroyed us. Instead of allowing his decision to rob me of this moment, I decided to focus on the beauty of connecting with those willing to accept me. There are people who will go their entire lives never knowing what I now know, and for the opportunity to know my family, I choose to be grateful. Though unsure what the future held for my father and me, I promised myself I would no longer be a hostage to a fantasy that may never be realized.

As for my daughter and her father's relationship, I recognize every relationship is different because our energy is uniquely different. It is not what she has with him that I wanted; rather, I desired to have what I was supposed to have as his wife with him. She is his daughter and I love that he loves her. I love that she has a protector and provider in him. Through their love, I am reminded of God's love for His children, and I am comforted knowing I have always been in His loving embrace.

Suppressing my needs and desires both in my childhood and then in my marriage was how I coped with pain and disappointment. I believed denying myself meant suffering in silence, submitting meant never speaking my truth, and peace came from an absence of discord. Here, in this fallacy, is where the enemy wanted me to live. Silence became how I attempted to control the actions of others. Being liked and creating an environment where everyone else felt comfortable was more important than what my peace required. On the surface, I appeared quiet, undemanding, and easy to please, but the internal screams of my soul were becoming hard to ignore.

It was easy for my obsession to become anger and hostility toward my father for his reaction because what I desired was not rooted in love. It was rooted in what I felt I had to live without. I had to face the hard truth that I was jealous. I envied the life I imagined my sister and his other children lived. I was willing to disrupt her peace because of the resentment I felt for the relationship I was prevented from having with my father. My well-being was at stake and if not checked immediately, could have engulfed me in a cloud of despair. After all that I had accomplished in my life from a position of forgiving others, I was confronted with an area where I still had growing to do. Through the experience of finding my father's family and the initial rejection that I received from him, I almost lost sight of the overwhelming amount of love I already possessed and the celebration I enjoyed from my mom's side.

The enemy wanted me to focus on the positive that may have been absent from my life in a way that created envy in my heart and would eventually destroy me.

> **A heart at peace gives life to the body, but envy rots the bones.**
>
> *Proverbs 14:30*

Envy lies in not only wanting what others have, but also in what we believe is missing in ourselves. To treat yourself as low or to treat others unfairly because of what you lack, or believe they have, causes you to miss out on the blessings in your life and the blessing you are called to be in the lives of others.

While I understand my story is not your story, I want you to know each of our stories is uniquely powerful. God's glory is present and visible beyond the desire to live someone else's experience. When you encounter someone who directs jealously toward you, see it as an expression of a need they have that you have been gifted to fill by responding in love. Do not turn away in anger but rather speak your truth in love. Allow love to take its rightful place in the situation because love conquers contempt. Pray for manifestation of the peace that surpasses understanding and a restfulness that comes from God.

If you find yourself struggling with envy, recognize this as an area where self-reflection is needed. We all have our crosses to bear but remember we have also been called by God to live out love. See yourself the way God sees you and focus on fulfilling the call He has for you. There is nothing more satisfying than operating in the purpose and plan of God. Acknowledge the good in your life, the blessings and the opportunity to do what no other can; to be who God created you to be. The enemy wants you to believe you are inadequate and less than, but I am here to remind you that you are and have always been more than enough. You are loved and you are valuable simply because you are God's one and only, uniquely and marvelously designed YOU.

Still Waters

Is strength an indomitable ability to endure or a stubborn refusal to surrender? I have done both and received the same response, "You're a strong woman, Sharonda." However, strong was not a word I would have used to describe myself. Instead, I believe I was simply someone too afraid to stop pushing. Almost as if surrendering would send me spiraling into an abysmal solitude, I fought being still. As a child, I spent a significant amount of time alone and the anxiety created by that silence was often countered by my self-created busyness. But what exactly does it mean to be strong? The overthinker in me concluded their idea of strength was my internal wrestle between fear of failing to become who others thought I should become and failing to figure out who I wanted to be. I learned early in life that if I kept moving, I never had to choose between the two. I could fool everyone, including myself, by constant moving.

Is it strength or stubbornness to remain hopeful when every moment of every day forces you to believe that hope is fruitless? There are people in my life who would describe me as both stubborn and strong. Strength, and even weakness, can be found in both our actions and inaction. Not doing is still doing. Not responding is still a response. Strength is in leaving and in staying, in the holding on and in the letting go. What matters is your perspective.

Imagine the people of God as they prepared to cross the Jordan River. They had already experienced His great power when God parted the Red Sea in Egypt for their passing so one would think crossing the Jordan would be an easy feat to accept. However, I wonder if any of them felt anxious for what was to come or had grown content in the land where God had given them to rest. At that point, they were closer to the promised land than they had ever been before. But this miracle was for a new generation of people. Babies were born and people perished while God's people endured during the wilderness period. I imagine there might have been a few people in the group who lacked the Red Sea experience for themselves and were like, "Joe, we about to do what now?" or "Nah, Joe, I'm good right here." Believing more or even the best is yet to come requires a tremendous exercise of faith. A faith birthed from the testimonies of what God previously brought their ancestors out of. It is in the stories of our ancestors, and our own testimonies of redemption and restoration that we understand how God's saving grace abounds.

We have to be strong and of good courage, knowing what God has done for others, He will manifest in our lives as well. I have many examples to draw from and yet I will confess to you that I still have my moments where I cry out, why me Lord? Why save me from the things of my past only for me to suffer now? Why bring me this far only to endure more pain and heartbreak? It is in those moments that I revisit the story of God's people and the miracle of reaching the promised land. After crossing the Jordan River, conquering Canaan and the fall of Jericho, the people of God began to experience defeat. The prophet cried out to God asking why did He bring them over Jordan just to deliver them to the hands of the enemy.

Joshua questioned whether they should have been content to remain on the other side of the river, where they found rest. I have been there, at those crossroads, many times. Each time asking the question, why me or why is this happening? And each time I am reminded that in order to receive the answers I seek, I must look at my own life to determine if I am prepared to receive them.

Shortly after the release of my first book Nevertheless: Peace In Spite Of Pain. I was on a tremendous high from the success of not just writing but also self-publishing my first book, which I considered my "through-story". I was in complete awe of all that God was allowing me to experience from my vulnerable obedience. Readers took the time to share how my book was an inspiration and prompted them to face the topics of abuse and abandonment in their own lives. I was blessed each time someone shared how my story helped them to experience their own freedom and peace *in spite of the pain.* The overwhelming support confirmed for me that publishing my story of faith, perseverance, and hope was the right thing to do. Nothing could make me doubt my decision to bear my soul, at least not until I received the call that would challenge everything I thought I believed.

It was the afternoon of December 20, 2017. My phone rang and on the other end I heard, "MJ, I need to talk to you." MJ was the nickname my son Donaven gave me. It was short for Mama Jones. Only he and his closest friends called me MJ so I knew the voice. It was his ex-girlfriend with whom I had grown close and still considered like a daughter even though their relationship had ended.

"What's wrong?" I asked her, but she refused to tell me. She would only say she needed to tell me something face to face. I asked her if she was pregnant and silently praised God when she answered no. I remember thinking if she said yes, how I was going to ring my son's neck from that day until the day the baby was born. I was still waiting for him to respond to a text message I sent earlier so if he was avoiding telling me he had a baby on the way, I would also ring his neck for ignoring me.

"Stop playing Monica and tell me what's wrong." When she still refused to tell me, I disconnected with her and called my husband to demand he get the information out of her. He understood I needed him to serve as a buffer for what she was going to tell me because, at this point, I was fuming behind the wheel of my car, which is not a good combination for me. I tend to be a little heavy on the pedal so the last thing I needed was to be distracted from driving. When he called back, I could immediately hear in his voice that the news was not good.

"Donaven has been arrested and sentenced to a year in jail."

I almost blacked out. Considering I was driving over 80mph on the 495 Beltway, I am glad I remained conscious. Heated beyond belief, I called her back and demanded she tell me everything over the phone because the idea of my son being arrested and immediately sentenced did not add up. Having had enough of my own personal experience with the law, being convicted of driving under the influence and previously married to a man who pled guilty to multiple charges in a major racketeering case to avoid a life sentence, I knew getting arrested and sentenced in the same day was not the process, at least not in America. To add to my confusion, I did not understand why she was with him. If my son was in trouble, why had he not told me? I could barely control the anger, fear and frustration raging inside of me. I would love to say I fought off the temptation to curse and yell but that would be a lie. Hurt and afraid, it was as if everything I had worked, believed, and fought for, and tried to avoid was right there in front of me. The worst part was realizing there was nothing I could do about it.

Growing up in poverty in Washington, D.C., I witnessed young black boys choose a life of drugs and crime for survival. I saw what incarceration did to them, the effect it had on their families and how it changed our community. I moved out of those neighborhoods and purposely made decisions that would offer him a better life. Although I felt the decisions I made to work long hours during day and attend college classes late into the evenings caused a divide between us, I relished in our accomplishment when he graduated from high school without ever seeing the inside of a jail cell. Because of how I grew up and where we lived, this was a measure of success to me.

I met up with Monica on the side of Pennsylvania Avenue in Forestville, Maryland. I needed to see her face as she spoke, as if the movement of her lips as her words traveled from her mouth to my ears would determine for me if it was real or if this was a horrible joke. She told me everything starting with six months earlier when my son had been stopped for speeding on his motorcycle, driving 150mph in a 55mph zone. He failed to pull over right away, which added the infraction of evading, and unsafe operation of the vehicle. He was also wearing earphones under his helmet, which even I was unaware was a violation since I used to do the same thing. The tickets he received came with a requirement to appear in court to face the charges. Whether it was embarrassment or pride, or both, he chose to handle this situation on his own. Ignorant of the possible punishment for the charges he faced amplified by pride, he chose to keep this situation from me and report to court without legal representation. Unaware a ticket requiring a person to report to court carries the possibility of one year in jail, he thought he would simply pay the fine and be done. Making the decision to represent himself in a proceeding where he was unprepared, cocky and arrogant is a decision he will never forget. As the saying goes, the person who chooses to represent himself in a court case is the person who has a fool for a client. As a result of thinking he was a junior Perry Mason, though probably too young to even know who Perry Mason was, he was found guilty on all counts and given the one year maximum sentence. With his friends watching, my son was handcuffed, escorted out the back of the courtroom and placed in a holding cell, where he waited to be transferred to the detention center where he would begin serving his sentence. This was my son, someone who had never been in serious trouble, never been arrested, held a well-paying job and had recently completed the EMT training program at the local community college. A year in jail for speeding. I could not believe how helpless I felt.

When she finished telling me the story, I drove off in the direction of the county courthouse. At the time we lived in Prince George's County, Maryland and his case was tried in Anne Arundel County which was about a 35-minute drive away. Home to the city of Annapolis, the Naval Academy and Chesapeake Bay view properties, his decision to risk going to court in a predominately white county and without representation befuddled me. Some would say this is irrelevant but unfortunately being black in America still means having to approach the law with extreme caution. Crimes committed by young black males still, more often than not, carry heavier consequences than the same crimes committed by young white males. Youthful innocence tends to be a valid excuse only when one's skin lacks melanin.

As I drove, I yelled. I cried. I screamed out to God. The pain was extraordinarily great; greater than anything I had ever experienced. I had nothing to compare the depth of this pain to and therefore no reference for how to cope.

Why me? Why him? What am I going to do? Why allow me to bring my son out of the life I feared only to have him still meet the same fate?

When I reached the detention center, I called the courthouse in an attempt to learn if he had been transferred. The clerk who answered had no concern for my feelings or patience for my call. I told her I was trying to find my son but perhaps to her, I was just another nuisance parent who failed to properly raise my child and was reaping the fruit of my failure. Maybe she dealt with parents, friends, etc. looking for their loved ones all day long. What made me any different? To her, nothing. She abruptly snarked, "Ma'am I don't have your son" and disconnected the call. I don't know what possessed me to go inside the detention center, but I did. Immediately the memories of my past life began to flood my senses. In a flash, my mind had taken me back to the year 2000 and I was once again walking into the District of Columbia Detention Center to visit the man who would become my first husband. I remember taking Donaven to visit him and praying he would never have this experience from where my husband sat. I hated that the detention center waiting room was a familiar place for me, with its cold hard chairs, metal detectors, lockers, security doors, wired windows and a tangible air of despair and heartbreak. My chest tightened as I approached the officer behind the desk. I asked her about Donaven's arrival and she confirmed he was enroute, but she went on to explain that I still would not be able to see him. The visitation schedule for inmates was based on their last names and it could be the following week before I would get to see him. "Ma'am, there's nothing you can do so you might as well go home." I turned and walked back through the waiting area, past the lockers, chairs and now past the people who arrived for their scheduled visits with loved ones. Just as I crossed the threshold of the automatic sliding doors, my cellphone rang.

"You have a collect call from an inmate of the Anne Arundel County Detention Center. To accept this call, press one." I pressed the button to accept the call and held my breath as I waited to hear his voice. "Ma, I'm sorry."

It took every single ounce of my being not to lose it. I knew I had to keep it together to prevent him from losing it in front of whomever watching. I pictured my son standing close to the phone, unsure of what was going to happen next. I wanted more than everything in this world to take his place.

God, please help me! Help me help him!

"Donaven, don't worry, we're going to get you out of there." I vowed, though I had no idea how. "Keep your head up, do you hear me? And don't let anyone see this getting to you." I tried to recall everything my first husband told me about jail and how he had to conduct himself. I could not believe I was now advising my son with the same instructions. "This call will end in one minute." the automated voice interrupted.

God, no, please help me! I can't do this. I can't God. Please!

With my chest tightening as if my heart was being held in clamps, I tried to steady my breathing and control the cracking in my voice. "Donaven, you hold your own, and no matter what, watch everything but see nothing. Do you understand?"

"Yes ma."

"I love you son. You hear me? I love you no matter what. Nothing changes that, okay?"

"I love you too ma." Click.

During the call I paced back and forth, believing if I kept my feet moving then I could avoid losing my mind. I had to keep moving. Just keep moving, but once the call ended, my strength left. My legs felt as if they would no longer be able to carry me and I almost dropped to the ground, right there in the front of the detention center. I walked a few feet to a nearby bus shelter and cried out until I had nothing left. I took a deep breath and cried some more. I sat there for what felt like forever. Somehow it was comforting to know he was near, in the building behind me. I did not want to leave but I knew there was no reason for me to stay. I remembered his first day of school and how hard it was for me to leave him. Parents were prohibited from walking beyond the office, so I stood in the doorway watching him walk down the hall holding the teacher's hand. I cried then too. I knew he was on his own to handle whatever came his way while we were apart. Of course, I would be there in a hurry if he needed me, but it was a helpless feeling knowing my baby was at the mercy of strangers. All I could do was pray, hope and wait. As parents, we are required to let them go. Our job is to raise, teach and prepare them for a life away from us, not hold their hands through every situation that life brings their way. We must equip them as early as we can to face life with confidence, and dare I say, strength. He was now on his own, just like he was 16 years earlier when he walked down the hall and away from me to a classroom full of other tiny young strangers.

Slowly accepting the situation, and thankful for at least having heard his voice, I used the strength that was returning to my legs to cross the street to the parking lot. I unlocked my car door and sat inside. In the rearview mirror, I could see the barb wire fencing and high wall of the center. I decided I wanted to turn my car around to face the center but as I put the car in reverse, I felt the Spirit of God directing me to keep the image of the center behind me. I returned the car to park and killed the power. Resting my head on the steering wheel, I sat there in the parking lot crying for another hour and a half, unable to leave. I reached out to a sista-friend who immediately came to sit with me. She comforted me as I navigated through my sorrow and despair. The fear was overwhelming. My mind began to fill with every possible negative scenario and I feared everything. I feared something happening to him that would change him, change me, change his future. No matter how much I tried, I could not gather my thoughts. As I cried, she began to pray. Looking back, I know this was God answering my cry out to Him for help.

She reminded me that the same God who has brought me through the darkest moments of my life is the same God who watches over my son. The gift of her presence was immeasurable, and I doubt she will ever understand how much I needed her presence and prayer through my pain. Eventually, I calmed down enough to begin the work necessary for bringing my son home. Another friend aided in connecting me with an attorney who agreed to take Donaven's case without an initial payment. He took the time to explain exactly what Donaven faced following the conviction, and the approach we needed to take for the appeal. Unfortunately, since this was also during the Christmas holiday season, courts would be closed for a week and receiving a response to our request for an appeal would take longer than normal. Donaven would not only sit behind bars for Christmas but would bring in the new year there as well.

For the first few days everyone knew to leave me to myself. My primary focus was making sure my son did not lose hope. In addition to working with his attorney to pursue the appeal, I deposited money into his account so he would be able to purchase items he needed, kept my phone charged and by my side to receive his calls, and prepared to visit on the first day he was allowed to receive visitors. Second was making sure I convinced everyone watching that I was fine. I still had a book to promote, one where I emphatically declared that peace exists in spite of pain. How would my story fair if I lost sight of the very promises that I told people were available to them if they just believed?

The day after his sentencing my Godmother sent me a text message that lifted my spirits and blessed me with the strength to press onward. The message read:

> "Good morning Baby girl, both you and Donaven are in my heart and prayers. Be strong and know that this test will become a testimony to the trials and tribulations of life. You both are VICTORS!!! not victims. God loves you and so do I. He will never let you down. God's mercy and love far

> exceeds and extends far beyond anything [you] can comprehend."

I thanked her and told her the message really touched me. She responded that she had been reading my book, *Nevertheless*, and came across this passage. I never would have imagined it would be the very words I wrote the year before that would help to pull me through what I was now enduring.

On Christmas Day, I awoke early to spend time with my daughters as they opened their presents then I drove to see Donaven since it was a visiting day for him. When my girls asked what time Donaven would be coming by to open his gifts, I said to leave them and that he would get them later. I could not bring myself to tell them where he was spending Christmas, nor would I allow them to visit him. I truly believed he would be home soon enough. Now, all I had to do was not lose faith. Despite all that I had been through, overcome and endured in my life, this would be the greatest test of my faith yet. Later, God would reveal to me why.

Up to that point in my life I really only had to stand on my faith for myself. Never had I been in a position where I felt I had to exercise my faith for what was happening to someone close to me. My son was saved and baptized in the Christian faith, and I never doubted where he would spend eternity. But this was different. This forced me to question my resolve and whether or not I could continue to smile when I had no idea what the outcome in the present would be. I had to ask myself if I believed what I said I believed.

> **...that all things work together for good to those who love God, to those who are the called according to His purpose.**
>
> *Romans 8:28*

There I was operating in fear and doubt, questioning my faith while smiling and trying to maintain a façade of strength and courage. Basically, I was carrying around, in my hands, a ball and chain despite God releasing me from its weight and confinement. God revealed to me that this was not my fight. I made it my fight because of self-imposed guilt and uncertainty. This was all happening to my son. I was not the one incarcerated. I was not the one who would have to endure being away from family, who faced a year of bed checks, lock downs, visitations and suspended phone privileges. This was not about me and yet I kept crying out "God, why me?". This was an opportunity for Donaven to be still and hear from God, our Father. When I stopped crying over the time I felt was lost, I realized the blessing in the time that had been saved. My son was pulled over for riding his motorcycle at a speed of over 150mph. As a motorcycle rider myself, I completely understand the risks that come along with riding but add excessive speed and compromised focus, the risk increases immensely. I forced myself to move from a position of pity to one of praise for the simple fact that my son was still alive. He had not been in an accident or caused injury to another person and, eventually, I would get to hug him once again.

Now, moving from pity to praise was not a sign that I was content with him spending the next 12 months in jail either. I decided to prepare him for an early release. I wrote to him telling him how proud I was, how much I believed in him and reminded him that he is a child of the Most High God. I sent him a copy of Psalm 23 because of how powerful it had been for me growing up and I believed in its power for him in this moment. During this time, my commitment to him was renewed and we grew closer than we had ever been. For the first time, since he was a little boy, I felt as if I had a new opportunity to be the mother he needed me to be, and finally had something worth offering him. I had my love to give him and this was the answer to my questions of "why" that I needed to receive. In this storm, I was blessed.

I was young when I first became a mom to my first born and only son. Still in college, 20 years old and living alone, I struggled raising him on my own. When he was a young boy, I sent him to live with my Godmother's mother, Toots, in North Carolina because I was working fulltime during the day and going to school fulltime in the evenings. I graduated from the University of the District of Columbia with a Bachelor of Architecture degree as a result of that hard work and determination, but I lost out of many of those early years in my son's life. We were reunited just long enough for me to meet a man, marry him and then leave that marriage two years later. I returned home but sent Donaven back to North Carolina to live with grandma Toots to, once again, give me time to get established. By the time I was prepared for him to come home, I was expecting another child and he was almost 10 years old. Two years following the birth of his sister, I was in a new relationship that resulted in my second marriage and another baby. Preoccupied with living my life, I forgot to make sure my son knew I was still in his and cheering for his success.

It was the realization of how little time I spent with my son that made me feel an overwhelming sense of guilt for this situation. I made his actions a result of what I felt I had not given him. Much of what I have gone through in my own life can be tied back to how I coped as a child. Where my mom struggled as a parent and the ways in which I adapted to her rearing is clearly identifiable in my life through the ways I approach situations and relationships. I learned to be a pleaser and made my sufferings secondary to the desire of others. I avoided conflict and ran from confrontation. The fear of disappointing someone who I thought was my only source of love and acceptance was paralyzing. Donaven's unconditional love made me uncomfortable and I faltered giving him the love he needed in return. The guilt I wrestled with revealed in me the similarities between my inability to love and my mom's challenges in the same area. Perhaps she too was tormented by the unconditional love I had for her and was ill-prepared, and too emotionally wounded, to receive it. I was now in a position to change the outcome for my relationship with my son.

While his situation was a result of his actions, I could not dismiss myself entirely. My role would not be to excuse his actions, but rather to help him identify the strength in him to get through it. It is the same strength that began in him as a child, when he walked down the hall away from me on the first day of school, was confronted by bullies in the alley walking from the corner store, or when he held my hand as I cried on his young shoulders and he told me everything would be okay. He could handle this, and I needed him to see himself as the anointed man he had become. My job was to love him through it. I had to operate in my role as his mother, nurture him, teach him and encourage him to see himself beyond his present situation. But I also had to acknowledge my part as well. He had been saved and given another opportunity to grow from this, and I too had another chance to grow as a parent and to draw closer to him rather than away. This test would become his testimony if he grew through it and the same would be true for me.

A few days into the new year, the lawyer called to let us know Donaven would go before a judge regarding the appeal on Monday, January 8. He warned us this court visit was merely an appearance, a formality where defendants report to hear the charges against them. The request for a bond hearing for his release while pending trial had not been granted. I heard the lawyer's warning but at the same time I did not hear it. At this point Donaven had been moved to a minimum-security jail farther away from us which changed his visitation days to Sunday and Thursday. I planned to see him on the Sunday before his court date, but he said he was not in the mood to receive visitors. He was losing hope about coming home and was beginning to prepare to do the complete sentence, which with good behavior could give him an August early release date. There was no way I was going to agree to missing our visit, nor was I going to allow him to wallow in doubt. I was proud of him for accepting the responsibility for his actions but like I said before, he and I have the same God and our God is mighty. I prayed with my son that Sunday and again over the phone during our talk that evening. I was believing for a miracle and it was a miracle I expected to receive.

After my call ended with Donaven, one of my friends called to check on me. She had been reading my book and was on chapter 14. As soon as she said the chapter number, I knew exactly where our talk was going. In chapter 14 of *Nevertheless: Peace In Spite Of Pain*, I share how God moved during the adoption of my daughter by my second husband. There were moments during those proceedings when I became anxious about the outcome. I felt alone because we had no family with us, and our attorney had not been as forthcoming with information as I would have liked. I felt as if we were going into it with blinders on. I had to have faith that God hears my prayers, and He did. What we did not know was our pastor and his family were at the courthouse for an adoption as well. When I saw him, I knew I was not alone. God was always in control. My friend reminded me if God did it before, He would do it again. Once again, I was blessed by something I had written months before. What I thought was for others was also for me. God was making a way and all I had to do was make room to receive it. The next morning, my husband and I arrived at the courthouse early. I located the courtroom for Donaven's case and walked up to the door. It was locked so I placed my hand on the solid wood, looked at my husband and said, "Let's pray." He asked me if we were *really* going to do this. Did he *really* think I was playing?

I thanked God for everything that had been done on my son's behalf. I prayed for him, the judge, and the lawyers on both sides. Afterwards, I turned and walked to the benches and sat down. All I had to do now was wait. When his lawyer arrived, he confirmed this was only going to be an appearance and that the bond hearing date had not been set. He knew it was my hope for Donaven to walk out of the courtroom with me but wanted to prepare me for the contrary. We would only get to see Donaven when he came into the courtroom to hear the charges. I thanked him and waited for everyone else to arrive. By the time we were ready to enter, our friend pastor Jeff, Monica and Donaven's then girlfriend Diamond were present. When his case was called, we expected to see him walk from the back of the courtroom but to our dismay the door where inmates enter the courtroom never opened. Instead of appearing in person, Donaven's face appeared on the monitor adjacent to the judge's bench. His expression, to anyone who knows him, was the utter defeat he felt. Every ounce of hope for going home was gone from him. Neither of us expected him to be on a screen and I know this was confirmation to him that he would not be granted a release as we hoped.

It is here in the story when it gets difficult for me to share without shouting and running around the room. You see, all seemed lost to him but I began to pray in the Spirit. My eyes were fixed on the judge and I never looked away. I could see Donaven in my peripheral line of sight, but my gaze was on the judge. He read Donaven's charges and explained to him the procedures going forward. He asked him if he understood this was simply an appearance and nothing more. Donaven solemnly responded that he understood. I continued to pray. By this time, I was rocking back and forth in my seat. My husband went to rub my back as if to console me but I shook off his hand. I did not need consoling, I needed agreement. In that moment, as if time stood still, the judge asked our lawyer if there was anything else. "Yes, your honor, there is."

Okay God. Let's GO!

At this point, I am rocking a little harder, and my hands are clinched as tight as I could grip them. Our lawyer continues, "We filed for a bond hearing but have not received a date yet."

"I don't see anything about a bond hearing on the docket. Do you have the paperwork with you?", the judge replied.

"Yes, your honor, yes I do."

Let me tell you, it was this moment when I could have passed out completely. If my eyes could see angels, I truly believe I would have watched them whisper to the judge telling him to what to say. The judge reviewed the documents given to him by our lawyer and agreed to grant Donaven's bond. He gave a speech that I honestly cannot completely recall now. I know it included a reprimand to Donaven for speeding on a motorcycle, the importance of pulling over immediately, and how much he appreciated seeing the support of Donaven's family and pastor even for a simple proceeding such as an appearance. He stated seeing us in the courtroom was an indicator of the support Donaven has in his life and a testament that we would continue to encourage him to make better decisions.

Please know the judge could have sung *Mary Had A Little Lamb*, danced a jig on the bench and did a 10-point summersault in a pink tutu and I would not have cared. He was letting my son come home and that was all that mattered to me. My joy was through the roof and I had my God to thank for answering my prayers. When we left out of the courtroom I turned to our lawyer and asked, just to confirm I heard correctly, "What does this mean?" He responded, "It means go get your son." With that, I hugged and thanked him for everything he had done. The next step was the appeal which set for 30 days away. This time would be different. This time he would not be alone and will be prepared.

After everything was over, Donaven was given probation and our relationship did not return to the way it had been. Glory be to God. My confidence and my faith were renewed, and I would need it for what was on the horizon of my life. When I asked God in prayer to reveal to me the lesson in Donaven's ordeal, the vision that I was given was simply of the number 2019. Immediately I felt a sense of being prepared for what was to come. This victory for our family would be the stones from my own Red Sea experience, one where God made a way for me when I saw no way out.

What stones will you carry with you to remind you of the waters that could have drowned you but were cut off so that you could pass through? What are your reminders from all that God has allowed you to go through AND come out of? Understand this, no matter where you are today, God has surely kept you from the worse that could have been. While it is easy to grow weary, understand the temptation to faint is right before the reward. When you feel as if you cannot endure another moment, rejoice for the breakthrough that is there. It is in our praise where we see our blessing.

I know it may seem easy for me to say praise in the good and the bad, but I can say it because it works. I have been there, and I am here to assure you it is a practice that is worth repeating. Understand also sometimes the breakthrough is not the revelation you are expecting; sometimes it is the strength to continue onward.

When you praise in the midst of your storm, I believe one of two things will happen, if not both at the same time, your strength will be renewed or your blessing will manifest. Either way, in my opinion, you win.

Where Are You?

Ever heard the expression, "I get it from my momma"? When some say they get a trait from their momma, they usually mean characteristics like long hair, shapely legs or a curt attitude. As for me, among the traits I get from my mom is the ability to randomly pick up everything, move to another state and start a new life. Occasionally I wish I could give it back to her. The wide hips and occasional small waist I will keep. When I was five years old, my mom packed enough of our belongings to fit into two suitcases and left our Charlotte, North Carolina home in the middle of the night. Clueless to the reason behind why we had to leave everything I loved behind, my room, clothes, toys, friends and her boyfriend who brought me bubble gum every pay day, I learned not to trust what was coming next. I also learned sometimes it is necessary to start over from scratch rather than attempt to correct your mistakes as you build on top of them. Basically, knock everything to the floor and begin again, one piece at a time.

In 2003, I experienced my own knock everything to the floor and start over episode. It was not the first time I snatched the rug out from my own feet and sadly, it would not be the last. That year, my son and I were abruptly terminated from participating in the Department of Justice's witness protection program. It was definitely a shock but, if I am honest with myself, it should have happened long before. Nearly two years earlier, my son and I entered the program at the request of the United States Attorney because my first husband became a witness for the government in a major drug, murder and corrupt organization criminal trial. Almost immediately upon entering the program, our marriage began to show signs of distress, and, after an incident of domestic abuse, I decided to leave him.

Participants familiar with one another could not live in the same city which required us to be moved to new locations. From Little Rock, Arkansas, my son and I were shipped off to Houston, Texas and given new identities. Being relocated with my son to another city where I had no family or friends was more stressful than living with my ex. I felt more alone and often struggled with my decision to leave him but now the idea of not having the program supporting me was terrifying. My son and I had only been in Houston for less than a year before I received the call that our participation would be terminated effective immediately. For the last year and a half, the U.S. government financed my life, paid all my bills and provided me a monthly stipend to cover other expenses. The objective was always for me to find employment and become self-sufficient, but they understood the process of reinventing myself required time. Realizing the hardship termination would cause me since I was without a job and in a city where I had no family or friends, the agent assigned to us allowed me one last monthly stipend. After that, I would be completely on my own. I was officially at rock bottom and I brought my son along for this ominous ride to hell. Jobless, no education of record and only a few hundred dollars to my name, I spiraled into a deep depression with no idea how to get out of it.

When I arrived in Houston, my agent asked me what I wanted to do with my new life, what kind of skills I possessed and what career could I see myself in. I decided I wanted to go into law. Not necessarily to become a lawyer but the next best thing considering my situation. I wanted to become a paralegal or legal assistant. She loved the idea and enrolled me at the Center for Advanced Legal Studies in Houston. The curriculum began with real estate courses, investigative research, how to reference case law and ironically the importance of defending myself, even when those dangers come from those who are supposed to protect me. For someone who already had trust issues, and trusted the wrong people for equally the wrong reasons, it was difficult to train my mind to be suspicious of everyone I met. Finishing the program probably would have been great for me but without the financial support of the program, I could no longer afford it.

Although I had paralegal classes to occupy a portion of my day, I could not ignore how desperate I was becoming for someone to talk to on a personal level. When Mormons visited my neighborhood to share their religion, I invited them in just for the company. I eventually learned there was a church located in Missouri City not far from our apartment on Fondren Road. The New Light Christian Center was part of the same fellowship of churches that my home church, Spirit of Faith, belonged so I trusted the teachings would be in line with what I had been taught. In the few times I attended New Light, the Word of God began to minister to my spirit again. There was renewal happening in me. I realized my situation would never change without me opening my mouth and asking for help. Silence was no longer my protector, instead, I began to see it as my oppressor. Recognizing that I was not alone in this period of my life encouraged me to try my hand again at starting over. I began volunteering with a community program that focused on the children of inmates and enrolled my son in the Boys and Girls Club. With Donaven busy with club activities, I decided I was ready to find someone I could spend time with. It had been months since the move to Houston and I felt I was ready for adult company. I signed up on a dating website but not to find a match of the opposite sex. Brazenly, I decided to use the service to find a girlfriend.

Okay, let me explain. This was not to experiment with my sexuality. I wanted a friend and I had no idea how to find one. I figured at this point what did I have to lose. I came across the page of a young lady who I will name Tracey for the purpose of privacy. Tracey was a single mother, around my age, who lived in an area near me. She enjoyed going to parties, Zydeco music and eating crawfish. Throwing caution to the wind, I reached out to her with the first line of my message reading, "I'm not gay. I could really use a friend." To my surprise, she wrote me back and from there a friendship was born.

She took me to different clubs to get me out of the house, we babysat for one another and talked about everything. Her friendship was exactly what I needed. One night, after we dropped the kids off at a 24-hour daycare, we sat in the car outside the club enjoying the drinks we purchased from the liquor store. It was cheaper than getting drinks at the bar inside the club. Getting tipsy outside the club meant the only drinks you would need to purchase inside the club were bottles of water. This was our single woman safety measure. Averting a pervert's plot to spike our drinks, and with enough water diluting the alcohol consumed, we were more likely to be sober enough to drive home without assistance from that supposedly kind gentleman who claimed he only wanted to make sure we made it home alright. While we drank, I decided to tell her the whole story of why I was in Houston. Normally, I never shared with others that I was in witness protection. I feared they would worry someone was coming after me or that they were in danger by being around me.

After I shared my secret and everything that I had given up for a man who sought to destroy me, she turned to me and said, "Well, that's nothing. I have got a secret too. I'm HIV positive."

Immediately, as if every drop of liquor had evaporated from my blood stream, my high was gone. "Wait, what?" I said confused and wondering if the alcohol was affecting my hearing.

She said, "You heard me. I have HIV."

"Okay, so what does that mean exactly?" I asked.

She replied with a slight chuckle, "It means I have HIV silly, that's it."

Confused and slightly afraid she was preparing me for much worse news, I asked, "Why are you telling me this? Are you dying or something? If you're dying, please don't tell me you're dying."

She laughed. "So, if I'm dying don't tell you I'm dying?"

Not seeing the humor in the moment, I said frustrated, "You know what I mean."

"Yes, I think I do. But I'm telling you because I wanted you to know. No reason other than that. Since we're hanging out a lot and I see you like a sister, I feel like you should know just in case something happens to me."

I could tell she was beginning to doubt her decision to share her news. I needed to do or say something to reassure her that we were still good, but I also wanted to know how this would affect us, if at all. "What could happen to you that I need to know that?"

Growing irritated, she said, "Look, I wanted to tell you and now you know. Okay! Feel free to forget about it if you're going to get weird."

Sensing things were going too far from where I needed us to be, I said, "No, I get it. I mean thanks for trusting me with this. Now you know I have like million questions, right?"

With a slight and yet still unsure smile to indicate things could go back to normal between us, she took a sip of her drink and then said, "Go for it."

That night I learned HIV, the human immunodeficiency virus, is not a scary monster that should be feared. At that point, neither was AIDS, the acquired immunodeficiency syndrome. HIV is something that people can LIVE with; it was no longer a death sentence. There I was sitting next to a woman who had lived the last ten years of her life with the disease, and she was fine living a normal life. She had even progressed to the level of AIDS, which I learned is not a separate disease. It is a stage of HIV that depends on a person's immune system and the amount of the virus in their system, or if they develop an illness that takes advantage of their weakened immune system, like pneumonia. Although she was much healthier now, she was still dealing with the stigma associated with the AIDS diagnosis. This did not change how I saw her. We both had issues. Some stemmed from childhood trauma and some from relationship choices, like most of the women we knew, but in the end, we were still sisters on our own unique journeys through.

I asked her how her condition changed the way she dated and if it was hard to share her diagnosis. She admitted the risk she takes disclosing but said it was an empowering experience. Each time she shared her condition with a potential partner, she took control of the moment in a way that the man who infected her did not have the strength to do. Fear no longer controlled her and she inspired me. Tracey went on to recall how she contracted the disease, and how she struggled to trust people afterwards because she learned he knew he was positive and did not disclose. But that was not the hardest part. Tracey learned she was HIV positive at the same time she learned she was pregnant.

My mouth dropped. Now I had even more questions. But instead of bombarding her, I simply listened to her story in shock and amazement. Shocked at the mere thought of someone using love in such a deceptive way and amazed because of her level of calm as she told her story. That night, during our talk, I saw her as much more than a friend or sister, she was the source of strength and encouragement I needed to witness. Her determination and refusal to be held hostage by her situation was beyond anything I could comprehend. Meeting her was exactly what I needed and God knew it. I leaned on her much more after our talk that night. I learned more about strength and perseverance through her experience. I had to allow forgiveness to live in my heart if I wanted to be free from the hold my first husband had over me. It was liberating to know someone who knew what it was like to feel as if everything had been lost and yet chose to press forward to rebuild her life. I now had a guide to help me experience the same freedom for myself. I was ready to get my life back on track. That is, until I got the dreaded call that this new life would no longer be financed by the marshals or the Department of Justice.

The reason for my termination from the witness protection program was because of breach of security, brought on by my actions. The U.S. marshals pride themselves on never losing a witness, so they take matters where a protectee puts themselves in risk of being found seriously. The rules of the program were simple – have no contact with anyone from your past and tell no one in your present who you really are. This should have been easy to do, but for us, not so much. While we lived in Little Rock, Arkansas, I convinced my husband, the witness testifying against an entire drug gang in a case making national news, to drive to Takoma Park, Maryland so I could get my hair braided. But that is not the end of the crazy. We had not been issued tags for our car. At that time, the dealership only provided a bill of sale and copies of the registration paperwork. The car looked as if it had been stolen. Back home in D.C., the only reason for a car to be on the road without tags was generally because either the car or the tags had been stolen. Both warranted being stopped by the police. There we were, two participants in the program whose names had been changed for our protection, back in the area where we swore never to return. Once we arrived at our motel room in College Park, Maryland, I called my girlfriend to come see me. When she arrived, almost on que, a helicopter flew above us with its search light scanning the area. To say we were terrified is an understatement. I am not sure who or what was going on outside our motel that night but it definitely caused her to shorten her visit and our plans of receiving additional visitors to be compromised.

He wanted to leave but I refused to drive another eleven hours back to Little Rock without my hair braided. Popular hairstyles for black women in Little Rock were not what I was used to and I told him I could not trust anyone there to do my hair the way I wanted. I realize now how ridiculous this sounds but at the time, I convinced myself this was the reason. I was unhappy in my relationship, but I had no way of verbalizing it or anyone to tell. Perhaps I hoped my girlfriend would see how miserable I was and convince me not to go back, or maybe I wanted someone to find out we were there and free me from the prison I voluntarily committed myself. Either way, knowing how addicted I was to him and dependent upon his need for me, even if she had begged me to stay, I would have said no. He was good at begging, and I was even better at forgiving him and submitting to his desires.

Besides the unauthorized trip to Maryland, we violated the terms of our participation by calling family using pre-paid calling cards and having family send us money through Western Union using our new names. Having money sent to us was probably the worst violation of them all because we disclosed our new names and where we lived. Well, perhaps not. If I had to bet, driving to an area outside of Washington, D.C. was probably the worst one of them all. What if we had been discovered? What if the gang members learned of our whereabouts? What would have happened to my son had something happened to me?

There was no justifiable excuse for any of it and yet I had trouble identifying the dangerous cycle of dependency I was in, one that now placed my son's life in jeopardy.

Once we returned home, my husband used the trip against me. Whenever I complained about something he did, he reminded me of that trip and accused me of being spoiled and ungrateful. How could I not see his sacrifice for me, after all that he had done for me and risked for my happiness. In his version of our reality, I was portrayed as the monster, with my insensitivity and condescending taunts about why he still did not have a job or what more he could be doing as a father. He was the damsel and I was the brute in this weird spin off of the Beauty and the Beast fairytale. And to think, I pictured myself as Belle, the one who had given up my life to move on with the man who was misunderstood and feared unjustly by others. I wanted my love to change him and yet it was his inability to love that changed me.

After the termination, I had a difficult decision to make, return to Maryland or remain in Texas. Returning to Maryland was not an easy decision because it meant going back to the same people who told me not to leave. I would carry the embarrassment of having less than I had before I left home. When I left for the program, I had recently graduated from the University of the District of Columbia with a degree in architecture and was enrolled at the University of Detroit Mercy to continue my education and become a licensed architect. In fact, I was already living on campus in Detroit when I received the call that we had been accepted into the program. My ex called collect begging me not to change my mind. The program had taken longer than I anticipated which was why I moved forward with enrolling mid-year. We married that January to secure my eligibility to enter the program, but my life had been on hold long enough. A few weeks before our courthouse nuptials, I rented a U-Haul truck and drove from D.C. to Detroit to report to school. I remember thinking how dreary and bleak the city looked with snow grey from car exhausts and road debris. The buildings appeared worn and old, and the people I passed all shared an indifferent stare, unmoved by the lack of color and vibrancy that I was used to and already beginning to miss from back home. I did not want to give Detroit a chance to impress me because I was afraid I would realize my life could be better there.

Not surprised to find that my dorm room consisted of a set of bunkbeds, but dismayed that my roommate had chosen the bottom bunk. This meant each night, at 25 years old, I would have to climb up into a top bunk to get some rest. Part of me was happy to oblige my husband's request that I drop out of school and runaway with him to a land unknown. One month after I moved in, I prepared to move out. I paid for six months at local storage rental facility and told my roommate she could have both beds. It took me about a week to get my affairs in order, drive to North Carolina to pick up my son from grandma Toots, who was caring for him while I was in school in Detroit. After I sold my car and packed as much of our permitted belongings that would fit into two suitcases, we reported to the FBI building in D.C. to start our lives as Jane, John and little Jack Doe began. It did not hit me until years later, the similarities of my decision to pack two suitcases and leave the life I had known and my mom's decision to do the same thing twenty years earlier.

Now, almost three years since I voluntarily surrendered my identity, I was pulling a small U-Haul trailer back to Maryland with the few items I owned to restart the life I left behind. I sent my son back to North Carolina to allow myself time to get established with a place and job. Unfortunately, instead of seeing this as my opportunity to start my life again, in a familiar place and surrounded by the people who loved me, I grew more depressed by the circumstances. The challenge was recognizing the strength that I possessed in midst of the pain blinding me. I struggled to see past my flaws and faults. This was not the life I wanted for myself or for my son. I was drowning in self-pity and the only way to save myself, so I thought, was to find ways to ignore how I felt. I wanted to numb myself to the pain of loneliness and abandonment. I had lost control and I wanted someone else to pick up the pieces of my life and create a beautiful picture out of them. I wanted someone else to tell me the beauty their eyes saw in me. I needed to be in a relationship.

Having a man in my life to call my own, or who made me feel as if I was a priority for him was my drug of choice. While the desire for companionship, affection and human connection is not concerning, it is the oppression of one's desires and lack of self-care or self-esteem for risk of another person's affection or acceptance that makes the need unhealthy. I needed to be needed, wanted to be wanted, and was willing to give up my life for someone who promised to need and want me. In Robin Norwood's book, *Women Who Love Too Much*, I could relate to many of the characteristics listed that were signs for concern: my needs were not met as a child, I became a pseudo caregiver to men who I felt lacked love, was willing to try harder or give more to keep a relationship, and I was more comfortable with suffering than being at peace. I was an intelligent and beautiful yet broken and bruised woman.

The idea of focusing my attention on my own insufficiencies sent my anxiety into overdrive. It was easier to settle my focus on performing for acceptance by others than trying to learn how to accept myself. To feed my addiction for attention, I welcomed lust back into my life. I used sex to experience intimacy and hoped intimacy would lead to commitment. I returned to what was familiar to me. Similar to a recovering drug addict who convinces themselves that one hit does not constitute a relapse. When I felt unloved and unlovable, I would become caught up in a web of lies that once held me in bondage emotionally as a teenager looking for love in abusive relationships. The difference now was that I was an adult and should have known better. Now to the complicate things, I managed to become ashamed of the shame.

I met up with Tracey in San Antonio, Texas a few years later. It was wonderful to see her again and catch up. I had much to share with her and wanted her to see for herself that I was in a better mental space. Well, I wanted her to believe I was anyway. I would only share that I had a great job, my own place and even had another child. I would keep the part about spiraling down a dark hole emotionally, getting arrested for drunk driving, being rejected by my second child's father or briefly trying my hand at becoming an exotic dancer to myself. I figured, why bore her with the details. We decided to meet for dinner. As soon as I saw her, I knew something was different. Her step was livelier, and her smile was bigger and brighter than ever before. As she approached me for an embraced, she held up her hand and I instantly saw the source of her joy. She was married and the ring was beautiful but all I could wonder was, *how*?

Tracey started to tell me everything about her new love. She said they met at a party. She thought he was walking up to her but he was actually walking to the table that held the food. He reached for a plate and said hello.

From there, the typical boy meets girl scenario played out and they exchanged numbers. He was single, no children and had a good job. I said, "the trifecta" and we both laughed. They danced, laughed, and talked all night. I could tell she enjoyed going down memory lane because of how much her face lit up as she recalled the details. I was happy for her but, deep down, I was in disbelief. I wanted to ask the question burning inside but I waited patiently for her to finish her love story.

She pulled out her phone and showed me pictures of him. He was tall and very attractive. They looked great together. I signaled to the waiter for another drink. Although it was absolutely none of my business, I had to know. Was he HIV positive too? Had she told him? What if she hid her status? I could no longer handle not knowing. As soon as my drink arrived, I took a big swallow and said, "Does he know?"

"Yes," she said and then added, "and he's negative."

Wait, what? How?

I realized by then HIV/AIDS had been around for almost thirty years but there was still a great deal of negative stigma about the disease, especially in the black community. Being HIV positive was still not widely accepted and most kept their status secret. Blacks not only avoided telling others, but they avoided knowing for themselves, which contributed to the constantly increasing rate of infections, especially among teens. Men who disclosed their status were automatically assumed to be homosexual or on the downlow and girls dreaded being classified as the chick with death between her legs. Unmoved by the plight of HIV on their community, they continued to engage in unprotected sex to maintain the appearance of being disease-free while the entire time, infecting others with the disease they feared the most. Living in fear of someone finding out their status meant they delayed starting the medications they desperately needed. This cycle is one of the reasons the disease continues to thrive today, in every community, regardless of race, sexual orientation or even age. Even senior citizens are at risk. With the advancements in medications to extend the sex drive and stamina, the elderly are among the rising groups of persons infected with HIV. In addition to having talk about using protection with teens, we may need to have a similar talk with grandma and grandpa.

Tracey and her husband's first official date was to church and then brunch afterwards. At this point I figured she was lying. She wanted me to believe she met a man, who then went to church with her, accepted she was living with HIV and wanted to marry her. *Okay, what's the catch?* I hated that I was this skeptical and filled with doubt. I mean, she was beautiful, kind and smart, all great reasons for a man to want to put a ring on her finger but there I was, still single and desperate. Clearly, I was jealous.

Just when I thought the agony of trying to hide my envy was over, she swiped her phone to another picture but this time there was a baby in the picture. *Okay,* I thought to myself, *this is enough.*

"Wait, you had another baby?" I asked, trying my best to sound enthusiastic and not cynical.

"Yes, he's a year old now." The pride, love and the joy of a being mom, wife and woman living her best life ever beamed through her smile.

Treading lightly so not to sound judgmental, I said, "I thought you said you were done having kids."

"I thought so too but he didn't have any children so I decided what's the harm in having one more."

Somewhat contemptuously, I said, "I can't believe you did it. And did it for him."

With a big, beautiful grin, she responded, "Yea, neither can I but I'm glad I did."

It was difficult to gauge whether she was totally oblivious to my tone or purposefully ignoring it. I knew she could have children with her condition so that was not the shocking part for me. With medication she could conceive and give birth to a child who was negative, she had already proven that with the birth of her daughter I knew in Texas. The rate of transmission for mothers who are on medication was much lower now than it was when she had her first child and with a cesarean delivery, the risk was even lower. What I was confused about was how the baby was conceived since transmission happens through sex. I wondered how he maintained being negative and how she convinced a man to wear a condom for their entire marriage when most people marry so they can stop using them.

Finally, I mustered up the nerve to ask, "So he's good with wearing a condom every time, for the rest of your lives?"

"Sharonda, true love makes a way and plus, he doesn't have to wear one all the time."

"He's not afraid of getting it from you?" I asked with more skepticism showing than I realized.

"No. I would like to say it's because he trusts me, but the fact is he's taken the time to educate himself about my condition. That's the best part. He's my partner not just in marriage but also in my health."

"Okay, you've got to tell me how though." By this time, I was on my third drink.

"Why, you plan to marry a guy who's HIV positive?"

If life was as great as she was making it out to be, I thought perhaps I should. Then again, maybe that was the liquor kicking in. I said, "No, but seriously, how is it that you two are engaging in unprotected sex without fear of passing it along?"

"It comes down to knowing your status and taking your medication. That's the part that people don't seem to get." She was an expert, which impressed me.

"You sound like a commercial." I said trying to laugh off my skepticism.

"Sharonda, I can only tell you what I know. When HIV positive people take their medications, the level of the virus in their body is too low to pass it along."

"Which means no protection?" I figured this should be the tag line for every HIV medication commercial.

"Yes," she said with a big smile, "fun times for all."

Forget showing people cooking and playing cards with family and friends. They should simply display a placard for 30 seconds that says, "Take your meds, forget the condom". But then again, HIV is not the only disease to worry about. This is why it is good I never went into marketing.

I left our meeting feeling conflicted. Where was I? What land of make believe had I stepped into where she could find a husband to love her and I suffered as a single? I was happy for her but I wanted a man to love me like her husband obviously loved her, deep enough to cover what could be considered a flaw or challenge. I took her blessing and the storms I had gone through since I left Texas as proof that God no longer had my back. The enemy is crafty that way. Like the cunning exchange between Eve and the serpent, God never told me I was supposed to have a life like my friend Tracey and yet I felt because of her relationship, that she was blessed and I had been forgotten. I was unable to recognize the blessings in being single. I was ashamed in my loneliness. She was where I wanted to be. When God asked Adam and Eve, "Where are you?", He did so to give them an opportunity in that moment to recognize they had removed themselves from His presence. The guilt I felt for envying her caused me to want to hide. My relationship with God and His Word should have been my hiding place, but instead, in my quest for control was where I often escaped.

Long before I married husband number one, I joined the Spirit of Faith Christian Center church. I learned of my Christian responsibility to help those who are less fortunate and to not judge them for past mistakes. But I also learned about submitting to my husband and being a virtuous woman. Unfortunately, the messages about marriage were being received by someone who was broken and unable to grasp the entire picture of waiting on God. Instead of hearing how to submit to God or to His Word, or how being virtuous has nothing to do with being married, I chose to rush into a marriage with a man I barely knew, who was already predisposed with legal troubles and unavailable physically and emotionally. Turning a blind eye to all the red flags that should have sparked a run-to-the-hills response, I saw him as someone who was misjudged and in need. Convinced this was best for me, I ignored his sporadic cruelty, and rested on the fantasy I had created for our lives together. In this state, no one would have been able to explain to me how my decisions were grounded in my need for control. As a new Christian and a single mom, I wanted to create this new life for this new creation that the Word of God said I had become. If the Word of God has the POWER to create a new person in me, why would I believe I had to take on the sole responsibility of building this new version of myself by myself? Although I had been given a new spiritual house, I wanted to move all my old furniture into it because I was afraid of how it would look to others if it was empty.

The circumstances of my marriage, separated from my immediate family, surrendered identity and dependency upon an abusive husband, were ideal conditions for Stockholm syndrome, often described as a means for survival for persons who feel trapped in abusive relationships or hostage situations. Manipulated, the victim or hostage begins to develop feelings for the person holding them against their will. Eventually, for the hostage, the line between their life before and their life during confinement becomes distorted as moments where the kidnapper shows care, concern and sensitivity start to outnumber the memories of their pre-hostage life. The victim becomes the caretaker and, if not careful, will begin to assist the kidnapper in crimes against others to show loyalty and dedication. Denial becomes a form of protection.

My love the care I extended to my abuser made me feel in control of my life and relationship. His incarceration was an attraction rather than a deterrent. The lack of control he had over his own life resonated with the lack of control I felt as a child. He became the replacement for the child in me that still longed for protection. Inescapably drawn to his dependency, I began to rely on him for validation. Protecting his feelings by any means necessary masked the loneliness, loathing and pitifulness that I felt about myself. Although I had accepted Jesus as my Savior, I lacked understanding of the Word. I was under the impression that once I accepted Christ, I was protected from future attacks, would immediately be able to recognize leading by the Holy Spirit, and my world would overflow with prosperity. Without spiritual guidance from others who understood the fight for my soul, I was not prepared to face my personal demons.

Now, back in Maryland, with the program and my first marriage behind me, I had to handle the extra emotional baggage that I collected along the way. After listening to Tracey's story of love and acceptance, I did not want to wait for God to position me in the path of a man to love me, nor did I want to relinquish control to God's Will for my life. I wanted to make it happen for myself. His Word and the testimonies of my past should have been enough for me but I refused to acknowledge my wrongs or how I stood in the way of my own my blessings. If I had to look to an example in the Bible for someone who took a similar approach to directing one's path, Rebekah comes to mind.

While she took matters into her own hands for her child, it was my future I tried to orchestrate a blessing over.

In Genesis, we find the story of Rebekah who, once barren, was granted the gift of children after her husband Isaac petitioned God on her behalf. She gave birth to twin boys whom she named them Esau and Jacob. The Lord told her the older shall serve the younger. What the Lord declared should have been enough, but for Rebekah, it was not. Favoring her younger son, she chose to manipulate her children and husband to ensure her son Jacob received the blessing of his father. Taking matters into her own hands, Rebekah made sure the blessing was done her way rather than God's and the consequences of her lack of faith, control and patience were inflicted upon her sons. With the same impatience and faithless haste, I entered into a marriage that perpetuated the dysfunction of my childhood. Instead of picking myself up and saying, I am the righteousness of God, blessed and highly favored, I looked for another dose of my drug of choice. I prepared to marry again.

If anyone tried to point out to me that I was repeating for a second time the same pattern of marrying from a position of dependency and low self-esteem, I would have balked at the idea. This marriage would be nothing like my first one, this one will work because he was completely different from anyone I have ever dated in my past. Normally attracted to the typical 'bad boy' personality, my second husband checked off all the boxes to be considered a 'nice guy'. He had a calm demeanor, was professionally successful, and had no children. He was not a drinker, smoker, or partier. His day-to-day activity was work and then home. He loved my children and wanted to become part of my family. He was safe. Rather than repair the damages to my emotional and psychological foundation, I chose to build on the cracks created by abandonment as a child and abuse as an adult. I convinced myself he was who I needed, to bring calm and security to my life even if it required sacrificing love, intimacy or passion. Eventually, like Rebekah, I learned doing things my way rather than allowing God's plan to be executed was a recipe for a hard way to go. The blessing over my life still existed but the road ahead would be filled with cracks and craters that held the potential to cause us to stumble and fall. And fall we did.

NO LONGER HOSTAGE

My Pleasure

Sex involves intimacy but intimacy can exist without sex. I almost lived an entire lifetime without ever learning the difference between the two. Adding passion to the mix, it was a fruit dangling far outside of my reach.

Those who know me or have read *Nevertheless: Peace In Spite of Pain* would agree that my teenage years were far from a storybook fairytale. Introduced to lust at an early age and sex in my teens, passion was a foreign concept until I was already in a passionless marriage. My childhood lacked examples of healthy intimacy, or comforting and nurturing touch, which in turn fostered opportunities for sexual and emotional manipulators to dominate in my life. The desire to feel a loving embrace and the need for protection caused internal conflict that lasted for years, challenging my ability to tell the difference between a healthy relationship and a predatory one. When someone told me I was beautiful, I felt dirty. When someone said I looked nice in an outfit, I worried that my clothes were too revealing. When someone told me I was sexy, I thought I had behaved in a way to warrant unsolicited attention. I was suspicious of every act of kindness or compliment extended from a man because of a subconscious depraved obligation.

Inappropriate sexual overtures were a constant in my life and I struggled to understand or comprehend the difference between true love and an overt need to be held. The demands on my mom as a single parent prevented her hindered her ability to protect me from the negative influences of the low-income neighborhoods we called home. From wanton interactions on display in my community as drug addicts performed for their next fix, to me wanting to fit in with the girls who were sexually active, I often chose the unhealthy form of affection over no affection at all. The deeper I delved into what I determined was forbidden, the harder it became to forgive myself for my actions. This destructive pattern was difficult to break free from and led to teen pregnancy, abortion, arrest, depression, and the decision to cause myself harm. I did not see myself as the Word declares, fearfully and wonderfully made; the idea that I was the chosen treasure of God or that I had been called out of darkness to experience His marvelous light was shrouded by my ignorance. Darkness was all around me and I was blind to a way out.

While sex may be to some a liberating act, enjoyed free of an intimate commitment, I refuse to believe this was the initial intent. As with many things created by God and then perverted by man, sex outside of trust and vulnerability is merely an attempt to quench a ravenous thirst for pleasure. A freedom that not only permits but encourages expression of lustful behavior robs us of our core need for a healthy form of intimacy. It was easier to give into physical desires and ignore my need for companionship. But as my relationship with Christ grew stronger, I struggled with succumbing to the whims of the flesh. A life of indiscriminate sex was not the life I desired but I was unsure I had the strength or courage to remove from my life a source of indulgence. Eventually, I decided the only solution for protecting myself and ending the debauchery that had become my reality was to marry, and to marry quickly. Both of my previous marriages occurred within months of meeting because I did not trust myself to be single or alone.

Unlike most of my childhood friends, I grew up in an environment where the topic of sex or sexual energy, the idea of a man marrying a young girl under the age of sixteen, or taking more than one woman as his wife were not taboo subjects. The idea of purity or saving myself for marriage was never discussed nor was it a consideration for me. Also contributing to my open view surrounding sex was the fact that most of the advice I received came from peers who were already having it. On one occasion, my decision not to wait for marriage seemed to work in my favor. In the car with my mom and her spiritual mentor, I overheard their conversation regarding the arrival of a friend from Ghana. She told my mom her friend was a prince and wanted to take on another wife, preferably an American girl. I pretended to be more interested in the scenery we passed but I listened closely for what would come next. With a motion of her head toward me sitting in the backseat, the mentor said, "Too bad she's not a virgin." I closed my eyes to hide my shock. My mom always told me I was horrible at hiding what I thought. She would say my face gave me away every time. I figured, if I could not see them, then they could not see my joy that I had given away the one thing they considered of value in me. Later, I learned the arrangement held the possibility of compensation for my mom had she gone through with giving me to him for marriage. To some regard, sex had liberated me. Unfortunately, this was a double edge knife in that it not only made me less desirable but it also gave me a sense of independence and control that I was not yet mature enough to handle. I wanted to be seen as an adult, but I was unprepared emotionally or psychologically for what adulthood had in store. As a result, conversations and interactions with my peers changed, attention from guys increased and the framework for how I would view sex, intimacy, love, and lust was formed.

In high school, I had a friend who encouraged me to use my shapely figure to coax material things from men. Although she lived with both parents, was adored and spoiled by both her father and steady boyfriend, she encouraged me to use what God had given me to my advantage. It did not help that I was receiving this same advice at home. My mom's mentor would often say my looks and my ability to satisfy the desires of men will take me farther than my intelligence. She believed, instead of devoting time to excelling academically, my focus should be on learning to use the energy of the Yoruba orisha Oshun, whom she and my mom believed was my guide in this earthly realm. Their beliefs and practices consisted of ceremonies to honor, worship and seek direction from orishas, who were assigned to intercede on our behalf to the supreme creator, Oludumare. As the child of the goddess Oshun, who is believed to be the orisha of love, beauty sensuality and even eroticism, I was often required to eat honey and bathe in flower water to appease Oshun's energy in me. Interesting enough, as an adult I still engage in those practices but for totally different reasons. Honey is used as a natural elixir and cough suppressant, and flowers added to my bath is a lovely way to unwind after long stressful day. It took becoming an adult to understand not all of my mom's practices were as voodooistic as mainstream wanted me to believe. When we close ourselves off to learning about the practices and beliefs of other cultures or hinder awareness of cultural differences, we are ultimately the ones who miss out.

It was this energy, or what I now understand was the ability to be confident in my own skin, that was missing from my life when I married both times. I had not yet figured out what I wanted, what made me happy or how to satisfy myself. I had not taken the time to figure out what I needed as an individual or to ascertain who I wanted to be for me. There was no one in my life to tell me that I could be sensual without having sex, or intimate without being physical. My confidence made me far more attractive than a revealing outfit and I could be respected for my determination and perseverance rather than by trying to maintain a superfluously rigid persona. What a concept. After marriage number two began to fall apart, I was forced to take a hard look at the part I played in things not working out for us. I had to acknowledge the difficulty I had appreciating him was a manifestation of trying to maintain a marriage void of the passion to sustain it. I wanted to blame him for our unhappiness but it was my internal struggle between a desire for passion and the suppression of it that was standing in my way.

As a teen, I used the lust men had for me as the means to a temporarily gratifying yet pernicious end. Bending to their lascivious desires caused my need for intimacy to become unbearable; what I believed to be my relief was really the source of my grief. A marriage void of the tempestuousness to which I had grown accustomed provided me with an unfamiliar sense of comfort and protection. He loved my children and offered me a level of stability that was new to me. I needed the calm he brought to my life and my children needed to experience the life that I felt he could deliver. It would take years to understand what I saw in him was the father I never had and longed for. Missing from my life was the unconditional and unadulterated love of a man, and I wanted to experience the care and concern without the requirement of sex. I was unable to open my heart or trust that a man could love me without desiring me in a lewd or lustful way. I was conflicted by both the comfort from the lack of sexual desire and equally the need for it.

In an attempt to make my marriage work, I prayed to God to remove the parts of me that did not please my husband. I wanted to like only what he liked. I wanted to learn to be content in a relationship void of thought-provoking conversation and intimacy. Unfortunately, at this point I had not yet learned about the pleaser and avoider personality traits to see the red flags in this prayer.

Although we had been married for over seven years and shared two children, one he adopted and one biologically his, I had to admit I had to work with great intention to be loving toward him as a wife. Our marriage was more like a friendship, which led to resentment and regret. I look back on the times when he expressed the desire to leave, and even attempted to leave, and wonder if it was worth staying together since our marriage ended anyway. In the end, I believe I had to be sure I had given it all I had to give. It was not my desire to be a single mom of three nor did I want to be a divorcee. This meant swallowing my pride, ignoring the signs that our bitterness began to overshadow our appreciation for one another and stay for the sake of my children. We both wanted to call it quits but neither of us wanted to be the one to pull the trigger. We were two people, holding one another hostage.

The failure to communicate and maintain the image of a happy marriage caused an unhealthy withdraw for both of us. We grew weak under the enormous weight of wanting to express our feelings without judgment or retaliation. While I have no proof of infidelity in our marriage, I can say there were situations where I felt disrespected by the close relationship my husband had with a colleague. Our marriage and the problems we were experiencing were often the subject of their conversations. It made me uncomfortable because I knew she was giving him the attention he wanted. I asked him to end it and even confronted her as well, but my requests were ignored. He claimed I was paranoid and insecure, but I believe he not only loved the attention but also loved the rise it caused inside me. Professionally, he was a top-level figure and respected in his field but at home, he lived in my shadow. In a way, this was an opportunity to punish me for not giving him the same attention at home; to dim my light so he could shine. The last thing he would do was give up the one thing he knew I could not control.

This made my brush with infidelity even harder to resist. At the time, I justified my behavior by the fact that I never engaged in sexual activity with another man (or woman). I felt this meant I had been faithful, but sex is not the only way to cheat. Deception can take many forms other than sex. It can be structured as private conversations between someone and another person other than their partner due to the possibility for damaging the level of trust in that relationship. This is why open relationships appeal to some. Full disclosure allows those involved to have a clear conscience, but it also opens the door to challenges in managing the expectations of multiple partners. Prior to marriage, being faithful was a struggle. I was constantly battling an imperious need for pleasure, along with strong sensual urges and the desire for romantic fulfillment. But in marriage, I made my vow to God rather than to my husband. To cheat on him would, in my mind, dishonor God. But when we started having challenges, I struggled to keep my promise. Especially when the old flame found his way to my daughter's school.

He was my first love that lasted my entire teen years. Our affair continued almost up until the day I met husband number two. I knew keeping him around, claiming he was only a childhood friend would be trouble. I was still physically attracted to him, even after all this time. Two of his children were enrolled in the same private school where my girls attended. Often our paths would cross, either in the afternoon during pick up or at special events like awards day or the annual family day cookout. Each time our eyes connected, it was as if time stood still and we were the only two people in the room. The memory of his hands touching me, his solid body pressed against mine would make my body quiver. He knew how and where to touch me since the first time we had sex. I was 14 and he was 18. Everything about our relationship was illicit and yet my body still yearned for him. The only reason I fought off the renewed desire was because I was married. His relationship with the mother of his children was not a deterrent for him and he made sure I knew it. One afternoon he managed to get close enough to me to whisper in my ear, "I need to see you." My body warmed and I knew I had to get far away from him. Although I believed engaging sexually with another man would violate my vows, I did not realize my desire for another man's touch was equally as bad. Instead of addressing it, I chose to hide from it.

Believing I thwarted the temptation to cheat, I shared my salacious yet meatless tale with a few female friends to find out if they have had similar experiences, as well as if they would be willing to overlook infidelity in their relationships. After talking with them, I had a different perspective on relationships and the options available to us to make our relationships work. How we commit to one another is not universal and is as unique as the individuals in the relationship. For the purpose of sharing their stories with you, I have changed their names to Margarette, Maude and Margie.

Margarette is not married but she and her partner have been a couple for over 10 years. She has been married previously but it was abusive and only lasted two years. I believe what she endured turned her against ever walking down the aisle again. They have one child together and both had a child from prior relationships. I often tell her she is married according to common law and that she might as well make it official. Her answer is always the same, "marriage would ruin us". She might have a point. If they were to marry and break up, theirs would join the growing list of marriages to quickly end in divorce after a long period of living together unmarried. Marriage changes some people. But I blame the people, not the institution of marriage. As for her answer to whether her relationship could survive either of them being intimate with another person, it was no and yes. They viewed infidelity as having a secret relationship or one where they had not been given permission to pursue. Since they both were allowed to engage sexually with other people, this would not be a problem.

Her divorce made her bitter toward monogamous relationships so they decided to keep their relationship open prior to living together, with one stipulation. She is bi-sexual and he is not. Therefore, she is permitted to sleep with women only. Both are allowed to see other women individually, as well as bring another woman into their home for the two of them to share intimately, but never another man. I asked Margarette how she handles knowing he is with other women, having sex and possibly developing feelings for them. She said it works for them because she understands as individuals, they may require more attention than either is willing or has the desire to give. Her position as quasi-wife in their hierarchical polyamorous relationship means the majority of his time would be devoted to her and any relationships outside of theirs would be secondary in importance. They maintain open communication and respect for one another's wishes and concerns, discuss all new relationship prospects, and are required to give the green light before either of them may proceed. For her, their relationship is anchored by mutual respect and the freedom to be open with their desires. She feels her relationship possesses a level of honesty and trust that many monogamous relationships lack, especially ones where one is practicing monogamy and the other person is not.

With that said, she might have a point.

When I think of their relationship, I am reminded of the movie *Professor Marston and the Wonder Women*. It gives a biographical account of the life of psychologist, lie detector inventor and Wonder Woman superhero creator Dr. William Moulton Marston, who practiced polyamory. He considered the women in his life to be equals. The women were bi-sexual like my friend Margarette, and the three of them lived together as a family unit with each woman bearing children by Dr. Marston. In the movie, which speaks to submissiveness as a provocative benefit in a relationship, the Wonder Woman character depicted a woman in a position of power, independent and strong. She chose to live as a subdued overlooked woman despite having the ability to outwit, overpower and dominate mankind. Dr. Marston wanted to show, to both men and women, the level of power that a woman possesses when she chooses to be submissive and the power of submission when based on love and empathy. Wonder Woman was the best of both, strong and submissive. As a little girl, I fell in love with Wonder Woman's power, independence, confidence, and secretly her sexuality. Of course, by the time the comic book character was presented as a Saturday cartoon, her characteristics and personality traits had been toned down significantly. She was no longer the sexual dominatrix that Dr. Marston created but I still coveted her appeal, power and ability to subdue while living a life that fell under the radar. Her need to fit into societal norms and the ability to secretly use her power to reign for the good of others continues to resonate with me today.

The movie presents submission in the context of strength rather than one of weakness. It is by the woman's strength that she is truly able to submit, and her ability to persuade and influence that supports her position of power and dominance. Contrary to the idea that the serpent of the Garden of Eden in the Book of Genesis approached the lesser vessel, it was her power, position in the home and ability to persuade the man that made her the target. Essentially, the woman should be protected because destruction of the woman means destruction of mankind. I find the idea of man who understands his position of protector and provider extremely appealing.

Next is Maude. She is adversely against infidelity or any level of relationship contrary to a staunch monogamous one. It is monogamy or bust with her but unfortunately, she married a man with a different perspective on the subject. Perhaps he supported the idea that she had to be committed and faithful to him while he would get to continue roaming the pastures of women willing to sleep with a married man. In the 18 years Maude and her husband have been married, I am aware of two indiscretions. One I had personal knowledge of and the other she confided in me when she learned of his cheating. The incident between her husband and me, I decided to keep to myself. Until now, that is.

I knew Maude's husband before I knew her. Connected through mutual friends, there were occasions when we would hold long conversations just the two of us but we decided long before he met Maude to keep it cordial. When he started dating Maude, she was added to the group without any issues. I watched their relationship grow from dating, to marriage, to married with children. I was honestly happy for the both of them.

One evening, a few of us were hanging out at their home, drinking and enjoying ourselves. It was comfortable. When it got late and everyone began to leave, he offered to take me home because of how much I had to drink. This meant leaving my car at their house. The alternative was spending the night. I dreaded the idea of going home and waking the next day carless, so I decided to stay the night. Maude agreed it was a good idea for me to take the spare bedroom. She preferred he stay home since he too had been drinking. I thought nothing of it until a few hours later, I was awakened to find him on top of me and kissing me. I could not believe this was happening. Was he seriously going to rape me?

"What the hell do you think you're doing?" I whispered partly in shock and partly in fear.

"I want you", he responded.

"You need to go back upstairs to Maude." My mind raced between an angry response that could result in a physical altercation or talking him off of this ledge. I chose to try to remain calm and talk him off of me.

Almost confused, he asked, "Don't you want this?"

"Hell no, I don't want this or you!" My voice was voice was slightly higher than I meant for it to be. "You need to get off me right now."

He got up, apologized and asked me not to tell Maude. I promised not to tell her as long as he never did anything like that ever again. At that point, my adrenaline was through the roof and I left. I had no trouble driving myself home. The next day, Maude called and asked why I left in the middle of the night. My friendship with him ended that night and I could not tell her why. Shortly after that incident he was caught cheating with another woman. I was able to explain my disgust and ending of our friendship on the fact that he was a cheater rather than because of his actions toward me. He had an opportunity to prove to me that it was a one-time occurrence. He failed and what I tried to prevent from happening came to be anyway. I had to stand by and watch her be destroyed by his actions. I wanted to kill him for the pain he caused her and for the guilt I carried for not telling her. But the last thing I wanted to do was add fuel to the fire he set to their marriage by sharing my experience with her.

Instead, I helped her pick up the pieces of her life and eventually they decided to remain married. I hoped he had changed his ways to spare me from having to watch her navigate learning to love and trust him again. Personally, I did not want her to forgive him but I knew she felt she had no choice for the sake of her children. It was more important to her to maintain the status quo than ensuring he was committed to her in the way in which she needed him to be. I wanted her to leave him, take everything and then light him on fire. But that was me then. Now, I would settle for a small simmer. She told me she believes him when he declares she is all the woman he will ever need. I pray he is telling the truth. I asked what if he ever cheated again and of course she gave the typical "I'd leave him" answer. I kept my response to myself.

While infidelity qualifies for grounds for divorce, Maude is like many women who have chosen to sacrifice her heart and stay in the marriage for her family. However, the decision to stay does not erase the hurt. If left unchecked, the person whose trust was broken becomes a hostage to the pain of his or her partner's violation and begins to look for a way to cope. Without true forgiveness, coping with the loss of trust can take on the form of condemnation and shame. To counter feeling confined by the offense, the person becomes the person who inflicts pain. Essentially the hostage becomes the hostage taker. By holding the episode over the offender's head, the victim now feels he or she has regained control over their feelings and the situation. The partner who cheated and apologized for cheating has to decide if he or she is going to live under the constant strain of trying to right the wrong, hence becoming hostage to the burden of guilt and shame. It is no wonder why cheaters are more likely to reoffend because the punishment seems unending. Forgetting is not a requirement of true forgiveness. Instead, true forgiveness requires a level of maturity to recognize who benefits from the act of forgiving. While forgiving someone for the pain they caused releases you from the hold of the offense, it does not free them from the obligation of apology through changed behavior. When you choose to forgive, you also free yourself from waiting for an apology should it never come.

Sometimes I wonder if she saw signs prior to the cheating event coming to light. Had he been cheating all along? What about all those business trips out of town? If he was daring enough to make a move on me while she was upstairs, what else was he willing to do? I decided the level of risk that he took that night was not something new to him. She had to have known about his waywardness prior to the incident she shared with me. It would explain why the expenses gifts, surprise getaways and excessive displays of affection stopped after he was caught. I pray he was successful in changing his behavior but if not, I pray she is able to decide from a place of freedom what she wants to do about it.

Last is Margie. Her story is similar to Margarette but unique as she is the only one who steps outside of her relationship. Margie is married and they have no children. Their relationship did not start out open but as a way to resolve issues of intimacy in their marriage, her husband agreed to her having a boyfriend. She kept most of the details about their decision to herself; I suspect this was her way of maintaining his privacy. She simply said he is no longer able to satisfy her sexually. It never dawned on me that people my age may experience a loss of libido or erectile dysfunction. I thought those were old people problems, but I was wrong, or maybe I am in denial about being a card holding member of the society of old people. Together, they decided not to allow his inability to satisfy her to be a reason to divorce. Listening to her, a wave of sorrow swept over me as I thought of her husband sitting home alone while Margie was out gallivanting with her side piece. But this was their choice for their marriage. Who was I to judge?

As for Margarette and her partner, they discussed how their relationship would exist prior to making it official. In Margie's situation, they came to this decision together to save their marriage. In the case of Maude and her husband, I am not sure where they stand since we are not as close as we used to be. I know she believes her husband is faithful but only time will tell.

Their unique stories helped me realize how important it is to identify and communicate individual needs within a relationship. What is expected or allowed if one of them is no longer able to perform sexually? What about children if either is unable to have children or is no longer interested in being a parent in the same timeframe, if at all? What about money, budgeting, and spending when one makes significantly more than the other? Throw in career choices, hobbies and interests, what if those interests are not shared or given the respect that one feels is warranted? These are all real issues for real people and yet some couples are barely able to discuss what they want for dinner without arguing.

What couples are willing to do to make their marriages work depends on how they view marriage. Is it an unbreakable covenant or simply a civil union subject to dissolution at the first sign of discord? I am still hoping for the former but that will only happen if I marry someone who feels the same about marriage and desires what I desire, till death do us part. I will admit, however, it never crossed my mind to discuss intimacy and sex to the level of these couples prior to getting married. I knew we would have sex but we never discussed frequency, eroticism, desires, or even non-negotiables. We limited sex to an act based on what we thought would satisfy basic needs and nothing more, not realizing how much of my past influenced my understanding of intimacy or sexual fulfillment. The baggage I carried from past hurt convinced me to discount the need to be vulnerable and, instead, attempt to substitute that need for extreme control. Out of desperation to escape the confines of lust and my own mistrust of my sensual desires, I entered into a marriage that lacked a physical, emotional and mental hunger. I truly believed if we simply went through the motions of portraying a happily married couple, then eventually it would become true for us. I was wrong.

Those considering marriage from a biblical position should take the time to truly consider what scripture directs in Ephesians 5:22-27,

Wives, submit yourselves to your own husbands as you do to the Lord. For the husband is the head of the wife as Christ is the head of the church, his body, of which he is the Savior. Now as the church submits to Christ, so also wives should submit to their husbands in everything.

Husbands, love your wives, just as Christ loved the church and gave himself up for her to make her holy, cleansing her by the washing with water through the word, and to present her to himself as a radiant church, without stain or wrinkle or any other blemish, but holy and blameless.

Discuss what it means for a woman to submit first to the Lord and then to a husband. As a wife, are you prepared to submit your body to your husband's will, desires, and direction? Are you able to rest in him as you do the Lord? Have you placed your trust in him to lead your family? It is important to be on one accord with regards to submitting, while understanding submission is not a position of weakness, but rather a position of love and honor.

As a husband, are you willing to love your wife through her weaknesses just as you do through her strengths? Do you understand this means never leaving her or forsaking her, giving your life for her as Christ gave His life for us? Regardless of her actions, her wants, her moods or responses, are you committed to providing for her as Christ continues to provide for you?

The passion of Christ is the measure of the husband's passion for his wife. He took on the greatest hardships for the church and died on the Cross for our sins. How do our actions toward our spouses compare to the love Christ gives us? I understand we all fall short, but this is not an excuse to avoid trying everything in our power to strive for the goal Christ has set before us.

Enduring a marriage that held us both hostage was like deciding to care for a wounded animal we encountered in the wild. The problem is the injured animal is afraid and wants to protect itself. Both wounded in our marriage, instinctually we wanted to protect ourselves from further hurt but that required trusting the very person we believed to be the source of the pain. We had to learn to trust one another again and over time, we learned having a healthy and mature friendship far outweighed a toxic marriage.

For twelve years, we managed to keep our true feelings locked away, we learned how to move amid our wounds and how to appear content within our versions of bondage. Eventually, I would decide to rip off the bandages and let my wounds breathe.

Excusing my recklessness, I believed ongoing lust would lead to a long-term committed relationship, and giving into the advances would result in love. When those choices failed to produce the relationship I wanted, I pursued the complete opposite. I believed I had nothing else to offer and there was nothing about me someone could learn to appreciate. What was I bringing to the table other than dependency? Love requires trust, affection, acceptance, vulnerability, sincerity compassion and empathy, none of which were familiar to me. Lust only required my willingness to be or do what another person wanted, that was easy. Giving and receiving unconditional love was not. Love gives room for people to grow and share one another's dreams and rewards, while having patience and understanding for each other's shortcomings. Lust, to the contrary, only sees what will bring momentary satisfaction or pleasure.

I needed time to sit with myself and in 2020, I received it. As the world endured the coronavirus pandemic, I came face to face with the harsh realities of marriage, family, self-esteem and the limits I placed on myself as a response to fear. During this time, I was able to sit with the version of me that I had become, to remove the pieces that no longer served my growth and kept me bound to the pains of my past. I had to acknowledge the ways I had grown, the insecure tendencies that framed my decisions, my likes and dislikes, the beauty of my wild and passionate side, as well as the desirable unassuming nature that draws people in. I had to see the beauty in my ability to survive, persevere, and nurture those in my circle as well as my commitment to protect those who depended on my strength.

It was important that I discover all the things I love about myself and forgive myself for the things I was less proud. I made mistakes but those mistakes did not make me who I am, my strength and determination did. We have all made mistakes, similar or worse, but it is our will to endure that makes us who we are. Never allow anyone to convince you that you must go through hardship to be made stronger. A person could easily choose to sit in misery, living in it day after day, without ever experiencing the strength they possess. It is when your will forces you to do something about your situation and your determination to act that you get to see the strength that is already inside you. What does not kill you does not make you stronger, you are already a strong, powerful, and purposed person. It only gives you an opportunity to operate in your purposed power. It is up to you to take it.

What I almost viewed as another raging storm in my life, God sent people to guide me to see the blessing. Rain is not a curse and when water falls in our lives, over our situations, we have to understand this is necessary for the flowers to grow and for the fruit of our labor to spring forth. I almost wallowed in the despair of another failed relationship without seeing the beauty of what my ex-husband and I were able to accomplish during our time together. Of course, I wish we could have figured it out and been able to avoid splitting up but there are many, many wishes from my past. I wish my mom could have been better equipped to raise me in a loving home. I wish I was able to decipher between healthy relationships and co-dependent ones. I wish my childhood included the loving protection of a father. I wish I declined going into witness protection. And I definitely wish that Jeri Curl of 1989 never happened. But without those things, who knows who I would be today? I cannot allow the wishes of old to keep me from seeing the beauty of my present or the hope of my future.

Pastor Sarah Jakes Roberts said during a service at the Potter's House that storms are meant to serve us. The Bible tells us how Jesus spoke to the storm and it obeyed. We have that same power to speak to the storms in our lives, as well as the power to receive what is necessary to take us to the next place. The winds are there to carry us and it is our faith that determines how we land. Rest in the assurance that you shall overcome and that all things work together for the good of those who love God, who have been called according to His purpose. Trust that you have been given a purpose by God and that nothing can separate you from His love. I know sometimes it feels like you are in the storm alone but let me remind you that your protector, guide and comforter is always with you. Your job is to allow your faith to help you enjoy the journey along the way.

SHARONDA JONES

12 Years A Wife

According to Proverbs 18, finding a wife is a good thing and can bring a man favor from the Lord, but there might be some debate over what type of wife would constitute a good thing. With both of my marriages ending, perhaps neither of my husbands knew a good thing when they had it. It is just a thought.

Not that it is a badge of honor, but I have experienced every phase of a relationship from single to married, to widowed and now divorced. A few years after husband number one and I were relocated separately to new cities, I learned he died alone in his Phoenix, Arizona apartment. Technically, because our identities were changed instead of going through a divorce, I believe his death made me a widow. But who knows? A small part of me felt sorry for the way he died, all alone. I imagine had I been there with him, perhaps I would have been able to take care of him and help him live a healthier lifestyle. Then I realize the guilt I feel for how his life turned out is typical co-dependency attachment. Our relationship was unhealthy and destructive, and for me to reminisce about it in any other way perpetuates the false narrative that kept me hostage for the time we were together and for years after I left him. As for marriage number two, we separated in December 2020, I filed for divorce the following February, and the divorce was made final in April. Who knew divorce could be fast tracked?

Before I moved out of our rental home, I never imagined I would miss being married. I thought I would be too busy relishing in my newfound freedom to ever miss that form of confinement. I was wrong. When I saw couples interacting lovingly with one another, had the desire to go on romantic trips, or found myself moving money from one account to another to pay bills, I would begin to long for a person obligated as my plus one. Then, before I could go any deeper into an abysmal loneliness, I would remind myself not every couple I see is a union of bliss, joy or happiness. In fact, they could be just as, or more, miserable than husband number two and I were in our marriage. How would I know if when our paths crossed, those bouncing balls of love and affection did not just finish arguing or were on the cusp of calling it quits? My ex and I were also good at portraying a similar façade when others were watching.

We met during the 2008 housing market collapse. The reason I reference the market is because of where I was mentally, which was stressed all the way out. I was an only fulltime parent, not to be confused with someone who is coparenting with another person with joint or shared responsibility, with two small children and earning less than $50k a year. The house I owned had diminished in value from my $217k purchase price to an appraised value of $45k. When I purchased the home, the broker convinced me to take a loan that came with a primary and secondary mortgage. I was delinquent on both. Having my ex come into my life at that moment was like meeting my knight in khaki slacks and Adidas sandals. He offered to move in to help financially, but I dreaded the idea of shacking up or having to explain to my children why there was a strange man sleeping in our living room. Hence, I asked him to marry me, and he said yes. For him, this meant giving up a three-story townhouse in an affluent area of Montgomery County, Maryland to move to a 900-square foot, three-bedroom, one-bathroom single family home, resembling a double-wide trailer, located in an urban area of central Prince George's County, Maryland. Let me put it this way, when he called GEICO to change his address, the agent said, "You moved where?" The agent then proceeded to almost double the insurance rate on his two-seater Mercedes Benz sports car. Not even my own flesh and blood understood why he would make such a decision to move into my house. When my son Donaven visited the townhome, he asked, "you're giving up *this* for my mom?" as if he would have said to heck with me, his own momma, and stayed put. But my ex thought I was worth it.

Admittedly, while I cared for him as a friend when I proposed, our two-month long relationship had not yet proven we could sustain a marriage. We were in essence still strangers, still getting to know one another and still trying to decide if we were right for a relationship. Yet, I convinced myself that he was the man for the future I wanted. Stability was more important than romance, and passion was for movies rather than real life. He presented as someone who would not rock the boat. I had already lived a life full of whirlwinds that swept me off my feet only to land on my face with nothing but heartache and pain to show for it. This time, I would marry for a different reason. This time it would be for the benefit of my family and not my desires. Unfortunately, I failed to anticipate how this decision would create almost insurmountable obstacles in our life together as husband and wife.

As a newbie Christian who had not devoted nearly as much time in studying the Word for single living, I was far from ready to walk in the union of matrimony according to the Word. Of course, I had heard my share of Bible phrases about marriage and the responsibility of the bride and groom, but I had no idea what it meant to be a submissive wife or to be loved by a man who loves me as Christ loves the church. I knew he had to leave his momma's house and that we would be joined as one flesh, which, in my mind, had already taken place a few times before we ever exchanged vows. I wanted a biblical marriage, one to make me virtuous and holy but neither of us approached the covenant of marriage from a holy or righteous position. I wanted this marriage to do something I never told him or anyone else; I wanted it to make me whole but that is not what marriage is designed to do. I was in denial that this marriage was the rebirth of a past relationship wrapped in my need to counter inadequacies. The abandonment that held me hostage as a child and young adult still had me bound. I wanted my marriage to free me but it would mean acknowledging things that were too difficult for either of us to accept.

The red flags began to appear almost immediately, but instead of seeing them as indicators of troubles ahead, I saw them as areas where I needed to work harder to maintain control. It was as if I was a doctor without an ounce of medical training or experience and our marriage was the patient, who happened to be dying a slow and painful death. There were times when I was able to give it pain killers for temporary relief, but the symptoms would return and the diseases caused by failure to communicate, lack of affection, avoidance and disrespect progressed. My patient's demise was inevitable. Without getting a second opinion or advice, the decision was made to cut the power to the equipment sustaining its life. While I do not regret getting married, I recognize we should have approached the commitment differently. Two people can be great individually without ever being great together. We were unhappy and it went ignored for years; pretending to be happy made it easier to blame the other person for our unhappiness. Talk about destructive cycles.

Neither of us had any idea the level of work, commitment, sacrifice or dedication a marriage requires, not only to the union but also to ourselves as individuals. Growth happens, it is inevitable. Growth can also cause a rift in the relationship if the level, direction or amount is unexpected or not well received. If one grows and the other remains the same, it could be a problem. If they both grow but in different directions or end up desiring things the other person cannot or chooses not to provide, this could also be a problem. For us, growing apart was not the singular issue, we also grew in understanding of ourselves and in what we ideally want in a partner. The only thing we had in common when we married was our need for a rescue operation, one where I needed rescuing and one where he was the rescuer.

Marriage gives but it also takes more than one realizes. Not in a negative way but in the way that a child takes from its parents or a change in lifestyles takes from what was considered the normal way of living. Marriage becomes its own entity and can only exist if two people continuously poor into in. It can produce beautiful fruit but it can also be used destructively by two incomplete and prideful people.

The day finally arrived for our scheduled virtual court hearing. I logged into the video conference meeting and prepared myself for what was next. Up to this point in the process, it still had not settled in my spirit that I would no longer be connected to the father of my daughters and the man I had shared my life with for the last twelve years. While I was happy the ending to our misery and the beginning of a new life was upon us, I began to wonder if our marriage would have survived if we invested the same amount of energy into staying together as we did in ending it. I sought counseling for myself and for my daughters. I had no idea how they were handling it and wanted to minimize as much of the negative effects of divorce on them as possible. It helped tremendously.

Therapy prepared me to address my attachment to struggle, for self and in my relationships. I chose suffering in silence as punishment for decisions I made in response to fear. I wanted to be fine, but I was still extremely angry with myself for marrying in haste, for staying in the marriage for optics, and for believing his definition of love was the only one that mattered. I was a hostage to my anger and I felt like a fraud. There I was, the author of *Nevertheless: Peace In Spite Of Pain*, straining to deal with pain, and floundering walking in peace over pending singlehood. It was a vicious cycle, and the only way out was to acknowledge my contribution leading to our divorce. My counselor helped me to understand there was glory for my marriage, even with it ending. I could let go of the anger that I desperately tried to hide. I learned to recognize the signs and unhealthy patterns of co-dependency in my life that would lead me to marry someone I barely knew. I married to cover the shame I felt for failed relationships, as well as an overwhelming dependency on others for validation and support.

For years I tried to force him to be someone I could fall in love with without ever trying to love the man he already was. I was critical of his every move, chastising him about the smallest things from his love of white bread or processed cheese to owning more khaki pants than jeans. My criticisms forced him to take a position of constant defensiveness. By the time I realized the error of my ways, the trust was beyond repair, at least not from the inside out. He was no longer willing to be vulnerable with me and everything I said or did was viewed as a set up or attack. The betrayal he felt and my guilt were the perfect combination lock securing me in a loveless marriage. I wanted to prove we could learn to be happy together and he wanted to prove I never would. Every argument rehashed the same "you never loved me" saga and each time, I withdrew. I kept myself busy with other priorities as the divide between us grew. With short periods of bliss, we mistakenly believed we could sustain our marriage, but the divorce proved otherwise.

Appearing on the screen alongside the box showing my face were our lawyers, my soon-to-be ex-husband and the magistrate. There we were, two people with our own issues of abandonment, not knowing to how to confront or love one another through them. I wanted him to appreciate my sacrifice to the point of changing and it seemed as if he wanted me to appreciate his sacrifice to the point of contentment. We were unable to see our life together as the other person saw it. Instead, it became easier to see the worst in one another, despite a time when we would have praised each other for our parenting and dedication. Now, we sat among accusations and insinuations that our children were not being loved or provided for physically, emotionally, or financially.

They say divorce can bring out the worse in people and unfortunately, I witnessed it firsthand. I am not proud of how we behaved and was surprised by how easily self-exaltation was able to overtake the mind. Viewing one another as an attacker affected how we responding to every request or statement. Had I been able to maintain a perception of love, honesty, and respect for him, I am sure the outcome would have been different. The Word declares we must bring every thought into captivity to the obedience of Christ *(2 Corinthians 10:5)* but facing this level of rejection from not just my husband but, also from my newly found father made it difficult. I felt as if the enemy had yelled "check" in my life's chess match and, thoroughly exhausted, I was ready to surrender in a game that I had already won. Love was the only way to issue the enemy a checkmate but sadly all I could focus on was the pain and disappointment.

Reflecting on how my ex and I were raised, it is easy to understand the ways in which we respond to abandonment. Both our fathers were absent from our lives, and although his parents were married, their marriage did not last long. When their marriage ended, his mom moved back to her childhood home with her little boy. He went from a two-parent home with his mom and dad, to a home filled with love from grandparents, an aunt and an uncle. I, on the other hand, grew up without ever meeting the man responsible for half of my DNA and who was unaware he had a daughter in the world.

The traits we acquired from our parents' failed relationships wreaked havoc on ours, and we lacked the clarity of mind to recognize it or the tools stop it. His grandparents and aunt received him with open arms. He received care, compassion and a stable foundation. My mom, pregnant with her third child after losing two children prior, was forced to navigate her path alone, while fending for herself and her child. She struggled with abandonment issues brought on by her mom leaving her in the care of a family friend to raise her, and grandparents who chose to care for her siblings and not her. My grandmother Doris Jackson had a total of seven children whom most were raised by her parents, Amanda and Lee Jackson. I will never know why they chose to raise some of my mom's siblings and not my mom but I can only imagine the pain of not receiving the same love and acceptance as her siblings was one that she carried with her always and eventually passed down to me.

My mom's past laid the foundation for my pain; my childhood trauma would then become the influence for my decisions. It was now up to me to, as my mentor Iyanla Vanzant, whom I dream of one day meeting says, 'do the work' of confronting those issues. To counter how I would normally respond, which was to leave, I committed to staying with my husband no matter how miserable we both were. If I was going to be hostage to my pain, then he was going to be held hostage as well. Once the divorce was granted, it was wonderful to finally be free.

While I was confident in my decision to call it quits, I was shocked that so many people felt the need to share their opinions about my marriage ending. Not necessarily because they had an opinion but rather because they were missing in action when my ex and I were up to our necks in relationship toxicity. Personally, I believe if a person chooses to sit silently and watch you suffer, then they can also sit silently and watch you pull yourself up out of the struggle. Perhaps they should also take notes in case they ever find themselves facing the same challenges down the road. One never knows.

How rude is it for someone to stand at the top of a mountain, look down on you and watch you struggle to climb to the top? Then when you arrive at the top of the mountain battered and bruised, offer their opinion about where you should have placed your hands and feet during the climb. I think this is one of those areas where my ability to avoid people is most likely a positive attribute. It is better for me to walk away from them rather than respond in the way my flesh longs to.

Countless times, after my divorce, I heard "God hates divorce" by one-book Bible scholars, apparently ordained and anointed only for the assignment of casting judgement on those who end their marriages. While I understand why they chose to quote a portion of their favorite translation of Malachi 2, I would rather they remind me that God loves me in spite of divorce instead. People are quick to condemn the choices of others, especially when they have not been forced to share in the burden. In those moments, I am reminded of how Christ dealt with the scribes and Pharisees regarding the woman who had been caught in the act of adultery.

First, based on His actions, Jesus was not the least bit bothered by their presence:

> **"But Jesus stooped down and wrote on the ground with His finger, as though He did not hear."**
>
> *John 8:6*

Once He chose to acknowledge them enough to respond, He said, "He who is without sin among you, let him throw a stone at her first." Then He went back to writing on the ground. To read Malachi 2:16 and then announce to couples struggling to find their way or to individuals who have made the tough decision to divorce is like standing on that mountain top and looking down in contempt. Wisdom is an important aspect in offering someone counsel. If one has not sought the wisdom of God, then it is best to observe rather than attempt to steer the ship without a compass.

By the time of Malachi, God's people had endured the big divide, lived in exile for more than two generations and were returning to rebuild after the fall of the Babylonians. They had been given an opportunity for redemption and restoration, but many struggled to remain faithful after all they had been through and where they placed their faith.

Instead, they began to put their faith in the people rather than in God. Sound familiar?

There have been times in my life when I can say that I placed more gratitude for the person who resolved a challenge for me or provided me a way out of a bind than I did toward God for being the orchestrator and waymaker of the good in my life. If someone was able to help me out of a situation, I was inclined to consider their way of doing life because I too wanted to be in a position where I had enough to help another. In a way, I made them the model for me to follow simply because they extended me a helping hand. A friend taught me all I owe people who have been helpful is simply to say "thank you". My life on an altar is not owed to them. Jesus already gave them that and He is more than enough.

The temptation to live as others do comes when that way of living seems to have more to offer. The men receiving Malachi's caution were leaving the women who shared their faith and beliefs for women who worshiped idols and offered pleasure without responsibility. Ask a man today why do men cheat and usually the answer is because the other woman does not complain, is available, and is open to do more to please him. If he was already struggling with his faith in God, in his relationship or his family's relationship with God, then a woman who will not hold him to the same expectations or standards as his wife would be a refreshing change, temporarily. Sure, a woman at the office will give her ear to another woman's man but she is not the one who has put in the work of building him up to the point where he is desirable to other women. Unfortunately, the one who sacrificed and offered support from the foundation level is sometimes discarded for someone who will reap the immediate benefits, without being required to commit the same level of effort. This is not limited to men only. Women are not exempt from leaning to another man when she feels ignored. It is this willingness to easily discard one another, regardless of the vows made before God that He does not desire for us.

While scripture gives the responsibility of the maintaining the covenant to the man by way of loving his wife the way Christ loves the church, and never leaving her just as Christ would never leave us, I imagine it is quite difficult for a man to endure staying with a woman he was never, or is no longer, in love with. This is where his faith must be activated. If he does not have faith that God can turn his heart toward his wife and his wife's heart toward him, then there is nowhere for the marriage to go. At that point, he will have no issue leaving the woman that he vowed to God to protect. Thank God for a Savior who will not leave the church nor will He get to the point of choosing to no longer provide and protect her. Until a woman fully understands the love of Christ, she will struggle to understand just how valuable she is to God and then to the husband God has for her.

The rest of Malachi 2:16 lets us know that the husband should do everything in his power to avoid putting away his wife or dealing with her faithlessly. Instead of limiting the focus to the act of divorce, it is the destruction of the family that displeases God. There are family units that are suffering because two people, who are not loving and even abusive toward one another, refuse to separate. This dysfunction causes more hardship than divorced couples who manage to provide a loving environment for their families to be enriched. It is not simply that God hates divorce but rather He loves family, reconciliation and forgiveness. As for what God hates, scripture tells us specifically:

> "A proud look, a lying tongue, hands that shed innocent blood, a heart that devises wicked plans, feet

that are swift in running to evil, a false witness who speaks lies and one who sows discord among brethren."

Proverbs 6:17-19

Perhaps, instead of condemning those who have made the tough decision to divorce, we should concentrate avoiding these acts in our personal lives instead.

I have been able to bear witness to my own personal growth and strength, and courage to wipe away the tears and press onward. When my first marriage ended and I returned home to Maryland, I was angry with God for not blessing the mess I had gotten myself into. This time, I praised God for the endurance to love and the ability to be hopeful despite how circumstances may have appeared. Finally, I understood how things work together for my good and the blessing in counting it ALL joy. Regardless of the dark roads I have traveled, the relationships that ended or the mistakes I made, I choose to forgive and to allow love to lead me. I apologized to my husband a few years into our marriage when I admitted to not being in love with him. I apologized again during our divorce. I decided I had apologized to him enough. Now it was time to forgive myself for not believing I was worth more.

No longer fearing being alone or single, I relished in the idea of planning my future and designing the life I wanted for myself. I was no longer hostage to unforgiveness, no longer ashamed of my past and no longer willing to place another person's happiness over my own. My life is what I choose to make it, not to be pitied and not be limited by anyone else's expectations of me. I would no longer be guilted into remaining in a situation that conflicts with my peace, nor will I ignore how someone's actions differ from what they claim. This includes me as well. I will declare what I want but I will also hold myself accountable to acting on what I believe and have declared. The abilities others possess or are willing to offer me will not dictate what I require. I determine how I receive love, and when I fall short and find myself accepting less than I deserve, I do not have to remain. I am and will always be the reward regardless, and sometimes because, of how much I may have endured to get there.

The same applies to you. You are the reward for which Jesus gave His life on the Cross. You have not gone too far to be forgiven. Each breath you take is proof that you have a chance at freedom and the opportunity to right a wrong choice. Choose to no longer be hostage to your past. Forgive yourself and walk in forgiveness toward others. Forgiveness is not a sign of weakness; it is a characteristic of great strength. When we open our hearts to understanding the plight of others, we extend the same compassion and consideration that we hope to receive on our journey through.

I recognize forgiving others for their actions, especially when those actions cause tremendous pain for us or our loved ones, may be easier said than done but I promise it is worth it. Choose to be an example of healing rather than hurt. Choose to depict the power of love, courage, hope, and faith not only for others but for yourself as well. Beauty and blessings are all around us but only those looking for them will see them. Love conquers because God is love. Envy, pride, infidelity, fear and unforgiveness can all be overcome but only by submitting to a power that is stronger and greater than the obstacles you face. God is that strong, God is that great, and it is God who has called you free.

Now declare it and receive it, in Jesus' name. Amen.

NO LONGER HOSTAGE

Epilogue

In letting go, I gained my wildest dream. By forgiving myself and others for the pain I endured, I was free to experience the greatest gift: love.

I found my aunt Patsy on Facebook, the go to place in my quest for finding family. I had been successful in connecting with family on my mom's side thanks to Facebook the year before. Finding her name along with others that I learned to be my father's siblings, I decided to send her a private message introducing myself and asked if she would be willing to connect me with my father. When the message went ignored, I assumed she received the message and elected not to get involved. This was the response I received from the rest of my father's immediate family. The fact that they did not want to get involved was not what bothered me. Their hesitation, I understood. I realized the potential for embarrassment and how uncomfortable it made them feel. I, too, was uncomfortable. The difference was I had been uncomfortable for 45 years, they had only been uncomfortable for a few months. The challenges I had with rejection, and abandonment were resurfacing, and the work I had done to overcome those feelings began to unravel. I felt the anger of betrayal rise inside me. I began to go through the stages of grief that were fresh as I was in the middle of the separation from my husband.

But Patsy was different. We spoke on the phone, and I updated her on all that had occurred the year prior. She invited me to her home for dinner, but I was skeptical. I explained my apprehension and fear that she would do as the other members of her family had done, which was meet and then never hear from them again. She promised this time would be different and she was right. She and her husband, Damian, welcomed me into their home and their hearts. When I asked why she chose to receive me with open arms, she responded, "Because you're family."

She knew at the very least, we were related even if she could not prove I was her niece. At the end of dinner, she said she planned to talk to my father on my behalf. I told her not to get her hopes up. Fortunately for me, my aunt Patsy's hope is in the Lord so there was no way I could convince her otherwise.

"I don't care if she's the president of the United States." My father was determined in his decision to remain out of my life.

Refusing to accept his decision, my aunt responded to her brother, "James, don't be that way. She seems like a lovely young lady."

"What does she want with me anyway?"

At first, I wondered why he would ask her that when he could just as easily call and ask me directly. Initially, I confused as to why my aunt felt the need to share is dismissive remarks with me. I wondered if she realized how hurtful it was to hear. I already knew, and had known for almost a year, how he felt about meeting me. By the time my aunt and I connected, I had received word from several other family members the news that my father wanted to remain absent from my life. "Give it time," they would say, "one day James will come around." Fortunately, my aunt Patsy did not agree with this approach nor did she believe ignoring the problem would cause it to go away. She saw me as family. To her, I was her niece and finding my long-lost family was a blessing rather than stain to the family name.

I tried to handle my father's response to being found by his illegitimate, long-lost daughter with a straight face but there were days when I was a complete mess. What had I done to this man to make he feel this way about me? Why was I not enough for him to want to meet me? Why did it seem as if every man in my life wanted nothing to do with me? I had to deal with my issues of rejection and dependency on acceptance before I could move forward in my life. I started the process years ago when God revealed the power of peace and purpose in my life. Now I had to level up and not fall back to the dark place of unforgiveness. I had to see my ability to love him through his pain, even if he never chooses to give love back to me.

> "…love your enemies, do good and lend, hoping for nothing in return; and your reward will be great, and you will be sons of the Most High. For He is kind to the unthankful and evil.

Therefore be merciful, just as your Father also is merciful."

Luke 6:35-36

His family was honoring his wishes. He was their family. I was simply someone related to them. The entire experience was a crude reminder that family is not contingent upon blood relation. Family is based on relationship and because of the friendships I have developed over the years, I know what it is to have family. My Godmother Barbara and her family are my family. My bestfriend Vinincia and her family are my family. My Godparents Elijah and Marilyn are my family. They have been present and accountable for over twenty years. God placed them in my life so I would know love. I was once blind to just how blessed I am, but now I see. And it is a beautiful sight to behold.

My aunt's faith encouraged my faith; the Word of God is redemptive and restores life to that which is dead. I knew she was right, but I also knew the rejection I had received from him prior. Thankfully, this did not discourage her at all. She was right, this was an opportunity for love to conquer. She assured me that she knows her brother to be a God-fearing man who would not turn away from me if he saw me with his own eyes. Her optimism missed me. For months, he hindered others from getting to know me. Their reasoning was that his health was poor and needed to be considered over my desire to meet him. It was because of his health that I chose to keep my distance. I already had his address, thanks to the ability to access public county property searches and at any time, I could have chosen to show up at his door. Never underestimate a woman on a mission with a computer and Wi-Fi. Now, here I was being encouraged to do just that, show up at his door. He gave the green light when he told his family if I showed up, that he would let me in. I decided to take him up on it. Patsy truly believed it would be a wonderful experience. Again, I did not share her optimism.

Flight, hotel and rental car booked, I was ready for the trip. I was also terrified. He lives in Texas, for God's sake. I imagined him pulling out a shotgun and shooting me dead on his porch. Extreme? I know. But again, I am talking about Texas. His home was an hour and a half away from my hotel although it did not feel like it. I chose to stay that far from his home to give myself time to collect my thoughts during the drive. I also wanted to be far away if things went really wrong. How do you prepare to show up to a man's home, unannounced, when he said he did not want to meet you? Well, first pray to God this is His Will and declare that His Will be done. Next, turn the radio up and blast Canton Jones' *Won't He Do It*.

I arrived on a Tuesday. Initially, I planned to drive straight to his house to get the meeting over with but by the time I arrived at my hotel to freshen up, it was already five in the evening. I decided it was too late to make the trip. God placed in my spirit to get a peace offering, so I went to a grocery store and purchased a potted plant. Cynically, I wondered if he would be willing to care for the plant considering he was not willing to care for me. I also bought a bottle of wine, which was for me. I still could not believe I was on this quest, a secret mission that only my aunt and her husband knew about. It crossed my mind that I was making a mistake, but I had to trust that God would speak to me the same way He did months earlier concerning the trip. Earlier the same year, a Black Girls Ride motorcycle conference was to be held near Austin. I made plans to attend and planned my route to pass through my father's town. I was going to ride my motorcycle to his house and hope for the best. I will admit that I had not gone to God with my plans because I was afraid to hear anything contrary to what I wanted to happen. I know I am not the only person who does this. Crazy how those childlike ways tend to creep up every now and then.

As I finalized my plans, I knew I had to stop being defiant. Too much was on the line. So, I prayed, "God, if this is Your Will, I pray all goes well and that You alone get the glory. If this is not Your Will, please Lord, let me know." About an hour later, I received an email from the conference organizer saying the conference had been cancelled due to a storm heading in the direction of Austin. It was expected to cause flooding along the entire east side of Texas, which included my father's town. Well…well…well. I think it goes without saying but I got my answer. I canceled my trip and decided to send my father a card instead. I imagined his expression as he picked through his mail, realizing I know where he lives. I choose to believe my first planned trip was canceled because God knew I would meet my aunt the following month. He also knew I would need her support and encouragement along the way. God is awesome that way, just awesome.

This time, I prayed and believed I received the green light. As I drove, I whispered a message into the air directed at him, "I hope you're ready James, because your daughter is on her way."

About a block from his house, I pulled over to collect my thoughts.

Sharonda, are you sure you're ready for this?

Yes. I am sure.

I know I am not the only one who talks to herself. Talking to yourself is not a concern, it is what you say to yourself that matters. I pulled up to his house, parked and grabbed the plant. I walked to his door and rang the bell. Nothing happened. *Oh goodness,* I thought, *did I just make this trip for nothing?* I pushed the button a second time and a few seconds later, I heard a click. The door opened and there stood the man I dreamed of meeting right in front of me. I will admit for a few seconds I wondered if he recognized me. Did he see himself when he looked at me? How crazy awesome would it be for him to exclaim, "Daughter! It's you!" Just as my mind was beginning to create this fantasy experience, he spoke, "Hello, may I help you?"

He had no clue who I was. As quickly as I imagined it, the fantasy was gone.

"Hi," I replied, "I'm Sharonda."

With part shock and equal expectation, he opened the door, stepped aside and said, "Well now. Come on in."

What happened next, caught me off guard. He hugged me. *Wait, what?* Is this not the same man who had proclaimed he wanted nothing to do with me? I stood in the foyer of his home dumbstruck. At this point, his wife entered the room and he introduced me to her. "Honey, this is Sharonda."

I extended my hands holding the potted plant to her and said, "This is for you." She smiled and I knew God had me in His care. Well, I always know that even when I act like I forgot. Arriving at their home with an offering of peace was not something I would have done on my own. It was an act of love and love will always disarm hate. He offered me a seat and we began to discuss why I had made the trip. He acknowledged having hesitations about meeting me and proceeded to ask me a slew of questions. I decided to answer each one of them although I could tell I was growing frustrated with having to answer the same questions his family asked me over the last twelve months. Had they not shared everything I told them? *This was ridiculous*, I thought. Was it possible that he was setting the scene to deny me to my face? Did I really come all this way for this man to tell me he did not believe I was his daughter? Let's just say, I could feel Phoenix, my alter ego, positioning herself on her perch, preparing to show up and light fire to everything around me. I decided it would be better for everyone if I left. A heated exchange was not what I traveled many miles at my own personal expense for.

I stood to leave but his wife stopped me. While he and I were talking, she was in the kitchen preparing something for me to eat. God, how sweet. I tried to excuse myself but she would not hear of it. Out of respect for her, and the weight this ordeal must have had on her, I decided to accept her offer. I turned to him and said, "My stepmother has prepared a meal for me and I am going to go eat it." I followed her into the kitchen and sat at one end of the table. He followed shortly after and sat at the other end. At this point, my focus turned to her. I knew what this had done to me, what his absence in my life did to me growing up and what his current attitude was doing to me now, but I had not considered what she might be going through.

As I sat at their table, I decided not to give the enemy anymore wins from this ordeal. God has allowed me to have what, up to this point in my life, was my biggest dream. The enemy would not have any glory in this, only God. I asked my father if he wanted a paternity test to prove what I already knew was true. He thought for a few seconds and then said yes. Honestly, how could anyone blame the man? The DNA results between his aunt and me only proved relation. He had no definitive proof that I was his child. I believed my mother, but he was not required to. I said, "Fine. I'll go buy one right now." I turned to my stepmother and said, "Want to ride with me?"

I chuckle when I think about how quickly things turned around. God is beyond amazing to have given us such power. Gifting us with the ability to love in the midst of pain is one of the greatest mysteries of life. Not because I question why He would give us such a gift but rather why we choose not to operate in it more. I wanted to react from an equal position of pain, hurt and unforgiveness but love would not allow me. Not my love for James, but rather my love for God and God's love for me that would not allow hatred to live in my heart.

As far as I was concerned, if I had been able to forgive my mom for what occurred during my childhood, the decisions she made out of fear and pain, then who was I not to extend the same gift to him? Sure, he walked away from us then but what mattered to me was his decision today. Did he want to know me now? I had to prepare myself for the possibility of his answer being no. But I also had to ask myself what if he said yes. Did I really have room in my life for this man, whose mere presence now reminded me of all that I missed out on? Did I really want a relationship with his children, the ones who were able to grow up with my father in their lives each and every day? Was I prepared to smile through all of the introductions, prepared to receive the stares and half hugs from those who struggle to accept me? Goodness, I did not see these feelings coming.

I returned from the pharmacy with the paternity test and we went through the process of collecting samples. I promised to send it off immediately and let him know as soon as I had the results. Since he needed the test to determine if he was my father, I did not see any reason to stay any longer. I stood to leave but wanted to capture the moment in a selfie. We laughed and took a few pictures to remember this moment in time. I turned to give him a hug, expecting the half hug I received when I arrived. But this time, the hug was how I imagined a father's hug would feel. He held me tight and thanked me. He spoke of the journey I had been on to find him and he blessed my return home. Things felt different. But I held back my emotions. I wanted the test results in my hand before I allowed myself to extend any more love than I had already given him. I thanked him and his wife, and I left.

The next day, I met up with my second sister who also lives in Texas. She had just learned of me during my visit and wanted to meet me. During breakfast, we connected like two kindred spirits as I updated her on all that she missed over the last year. Then my phone rang. It was our father. He called to thank me again for coming but it is what he said next that I never expected but always longed for. "Sharonda, I know this was God. With you coming all this way to meet me, this was truly God. Thank you for following the lead of God to come down here. I know we're waiting for the test results, but I believe in my heart you are my daughter and I wanted to say I love you. You are a wonderful woman, kind and truly a blessing. I am proud of you and would be honored to be your dad." Through uncontrolled sobs, tears running down my cheeks and snot bubbling above my lips (yes, I was giving full ugly cry in the restaurant), I thanked him for his words. I told him I love him and disconnected the call. For several minutes, I continued to cry but not out of pain. I cried tears of peace like I had never cried before. With my appetite lost, I stared out of the window and gave praises to God for all that He has brought me through. I realized my aunt had to tell me the things my father said; I had to endure the rejection and avoidance because without them I would have never understood just how powerful love is.

The fact that Jesus died for our sins is a major miracle but the revelation that He did it after receiving the most severe rejection and abuse is another. Forgiving my father and his family is nowhere near Jesus forgiving his accusers but I must admit forgiving them gave me a greater reward. My father was correct, it was all God who mended our way. It was all God who kept me and covered me through this journey. It was all God who allowed me to experience the lifting of pain, abandonment and rejection from my shoulders as I sat in the restaurant with my sister holding me in her arms.

Dreams do come true, and prayers are answered. Looking back to how I endured my marriage ending, my family breaking up and simultaneously my father's rejection, I know it was all God. Well, yes, I was in the equation too but without His Word guiding me and His children supporting me, I know I would not have been able to smile on this side of through. For years I refused to let go of a situation out of fear that I would lose what I sacrificed my peace and happiness to have. By choosing to be honest, forgiving myself and others, and removing the chains of pride that held me bound, I am able to experience more love than I ever imagined my heart could handle.

My trust must always be in God, for in Him, I am free.

ABOUT THE AUTHOR

Sharonda is someone who lives in complete awe of life. Mom, grandmother, mentor, biker and random try-anything-once rockstar, Sharonda chooses to see every moment as a lesson and conduit for whatever comes next.

Her debut literary work, *Nevertheless: Peace In Spite Of Pain*, is her through-story of overcoming fear, depression, abandonment and abuse. Purposed for inspiring others to overcome the pains of their past, Sharonda hopes *No Longer Hostage* will serve as a reminder that we are all here to grow, learn and love.

She is the founder of the Little Phoenixes Foundation, a non-profit organization that offers out-of-school STEM based programs for youth and mentoring for girls.

For more information on co-dependency, please visit
www.therapytribe.com/therapy/what-is-codependency.

Subscribe to receive updates or to connect with
Sharonda by visiting:
www.SharondaJones.me

For more information on Sharonda's
non-profit organization, the
Little Phoenixes Foundation, visit:
www.LittlePhoenixesFoundation.org

www.ingramcontent.com/pod-product-compliance
Lightning Source LLC
Chambersburg PA
CBHW020423010526
44118CB00010B/386